SMASHED

SMASHED

60 EPIC SMASH BURGERS & SANDWICHES

for Dinner, for Lunch, and Even for Breakfast— For Your Outdoor Griddle, Grill, or Skillet

ADAM & BRETT WALTON

HARVARD COMMON PRESS

Brimming with creative inspiration, how-to projects, and useful information to enrich your everyday life, Quarto.com is a favorite destination for those pursuing their interests and passions.

Inspiring | Educating | Creating | Entertaining

First Published in 2023 by The Harvard Common Press, an imprint of The Quarto Group,
100 Cummings Center, Suite 265-D, Beverly, MA 01915, USA.
T (978) 282-9590 F (978) 283-2742 Quarto.com

The Harvard Common Press titles are also available at discount for retail, wholesale, promotional, and bulk purchase. For details, contact the Special Sales Manager by email at specialsales@quarto.com or by mail at The Quarto Group, Attn: Special Sales Manager, 100 Cummings Center, Suite 265-D, Beverly, MA 01915, USA.

27 26 25 24 23   1 2 3 4 5

ISBN: 978-0-7603-8203-5
Digital edition published in 2023
eISBN: 978-0-7603-8204-2

Library of Congress Cataloging-in-Publication Data available

Design and Page Layout: Kelley Galbreath
Cover Image: Michelle Miller Photography
Recipe photography and styling: Michelle Miller Photography
Lifestyle photography: Colleen Hillard Photography on pages 14 and 140

Printed in China

This book is dedicated to our Dad, John Louis Walton, who showed us there is power in positivity—and to always keep our heads up and shoulders back.

Contents

~~~~~~

Let's Get Smashed!

Hello and welcome back to the WALTWINS Backyard Diner! Today, we're serving up some of our absolute favorite smashed and pressed recipes! From the first time we ever had a "smashed" burger—at the time we didn't even know that's what they were—at a favorite family joint called Ripples Drive In in Provo, Utah, we've been hooked on these thin, flavor-packed all beef patties! Once we learned to make them for ourselves on the griddle, we instantly found new ways to prepare this classic and developed a whole book's worth of smashed recipes to share with you! But we didn't stop at just beef smash burgers, we also wanted to include a variety of meats, pressed sandwiches and wraps, and breakfast bites we know you'll love!

Within the pages of this book, you will find a huge assortment of handheld culinary delights. We knew that if you simply SMASHED EVERYTHING, there'd be something for everyone to enjoy! From burgers, to burritos, to donut "buns" and more, your culinary toolbox is about to expand beyond what you ever thought possible. We cannot WAIT for you to dive into these pages and find an even greater love for griddle cooking!

We love the outdoor griddle and find that it has become the perfect canvas on which to create some of the most amazing dishes there are. It's no wonder street cooks have been using the flat iron grill to serve millions daily across the globe. With outdoor griddles now found nearly everywhere, anyone can become a world-class chef (even if just self-proclaimed) right in the comfort of their own backyard.

Family is important to us, and many of the dishes here may be considered "secret family recipes." But, as we always say, "When you're with the WALTWINS, you're family!" So now, we're passing on those recipes to you! ENJOY FAM!

If you don't own a burger smasher, we recommend a dual spatula method that results in a satisfying smash. Use the backside of the lower spatula to flatten your prepared meatball. Use the top spatula to apply pressure to the bottom spatula. You can choose to hold your top spatula parallel or perpendicular to the bottom one, but either way be assertive and controlled with your pressure and keep it evenly distributed across whatever tool you're using.

It is crucial that you hold it down the whole time. The pressure you apply is key to getting a good Maillard reaction, which is the chemical connection between the acids in the meat and the heat that results in browning. That's the crust you want!

We recommend holding the smash down for 10–15 seconds (but be aware it could be as short as 8 seconds). Once the burger is smashed and you see the juices begin to rise to the surface (almost immediately), use one of the spatulas to quickly flip it.

If you have a heavy weighted or cast-iron press, you almost never need to apply much pressure—neither for smash burgers nor pressed sandwiches.

If you have a thinner, lighter press, some pressure helps in creating a crust as well as getting a good toast on sandwiches.

Practice makes you better each time! It may not always be perfect, but remember, it doesn't have to look perfect to still be delicious!

Smash burgers are not "hype." If someone says it is, it just means they haven't had one of YOUR smash burgers! If you know, you know! ;)

Tools of the Trade

- **SPATULAS AND GRILL/GRIDDLE PRESSES.** Experiment with a variety of sizes and weights, but it won't take long for you to find your go-tos for every situational smash.

- **SCRAPER-CHOPPER TOOL.** This is a must for smash burgers, especially. If your burger gets a bit stuck a high-quality scraper can save it quickly.

- **TONGS.** A long-handled set of tongs is ideal for reaching over a large griddle or grill surface.

- **SQUIRT BOTTLES.** We've found these especially handy to have sitting near our cooking area. Besides sauces and dressings, we have bottles dedicated to oils and others for just water.

- **BASTING DOME.** This comes in handy when you're melting cheeses or trying to keep food hot before serving.

Pantry Staples: Spices

Everyone has their favorite spices for their burgers! Whether it earned favorite status back in the day because it was a family staple or you just discovered an amazing combination last week, these burgers and sandwiches are the perfect vehicles.

That said, we have found that salt and pepper always give us the best results! This is always what we have stocked in our pantry:

- salt
- pepper
- garlic powder
- onion powder
- adobo seasoning
- paprika
- chipotle powder
- hot sauce

Pantry Staples: Oils

Any cooking oil works well, again don't hesitate to use your favorite! We've used vegetable, canola, avocado oil, and even ghee and beef tallow. For smash burgers, however, it is best to steer clear of olive oil as it has a lower smoke point and can burn at a higher temperature.

BIG BEEFY SMASH BURGERS

THE RECIPES

Rocky Mountain Smash Burger

SERVINGS: 1 burger | **PREP TIME:** 10 minutes | **COOK TIME:** 4–5 minutes

This burger originated in the city we are from, Provo, Utah, where the Rockies are some of the biggest mountains in the world. And after piling on all the ham and toppings, the name fits this burger, and we're sure it will soon become a regular at your house. You can truly call this one a "Ham-Burger."

6 slices deli sliced ham

1 tablespoon (15 ml) vegetable oil

6 ounces (170 g) 80/20 ground beef, divided into two 3-ounce loosely packed meatballs

2 teaspoons salt (to taste)

2 teaspoons pepper (to taste)

4 slices American cheese

1 potato hamburger bun

4 dill pickle chips

4 tablespoons Fry Sauce (See recipe below.)

OPTIONAL:
1 tablespoon (14 g) mayonnaise, for toasting the buns

Fry Sauce Recipe

2 tablespoons (28 g) mayonnaise
3 tablespoons (45 g) ketchup
1 teaspoon dill pickle juice
½ teaspoon celery salt

Mix all ingredients well and serve!

1 Turn the griddle on to medium/high to high heat (above 400°F [200°C]).

2 Lay the ham on the griddle, brown each side for about a minute, and then pull and set aside.

3 Once the griddle is to temperature, lay the oil on the griddle.

4 Place the 2 meatballs in the oil, ensuring space between the meatballs to give them room to be smashed.

5 Sprinkle salt and pepper liberally on the meatballs.

6 After about 30 seconds, smash each meatball all the way down flat with a burger smasher or the back side of the spatula, using the back side of another spatula to help apply pressure. Hold the smash down for 10–15 seconds.

7 Once each burger is smashed and you see the juices begin to rise to the surface (almost immediately), use the spatula and quickly flip them and place a slice of American cheese on each burger.

8 Pull each burger from the heat. The cheese will continue to melt while building the burger.

9 Place the burgers, stacking one on top of the other, and place on the bottom bun. Build in the following order: bottom bun, smash burger patties, ham, pickle chips. Spread the Fry Sauce on the inside of the top bun and place on top of the burger. Serve and enjoy!

Oklahoma Onion Smash Burger

SERVINGS: 1 burger | **PREP TIME:** 10 minutes | **COOK TIME:** 4 minutes

Here's the smash burger that will have you singing O-K-L-A-H-O-M-A! This is a twist on our Classic WALTWINS Diner Smash Burger with the amazing zing from the onions! Steaming the top bun while the beef cooks atop the onions gives this one a depth of flavor that will have everyone asking for more.

1 tablespoon (15 ml) vegetable oil

6–7 ounces (170 to 200 g) 80/20 ground beef, divided into 2 loose meatballs

2 teaspoons salt (to taste)

2 teaspoons pepper (to taste)

1 small/medium yellow onion, very thinly sliced

2 slices American cheese

1 artisan bun

Toppings of your choice

OPTIONAL:
1 tablespoon (14 g) mayonnaise, for toasting the buns

If toasting the buns: While the griddle is coming up to temperature, spread the mayonnaise on the inside of the top and bottom buns and lay them on the griddle facedown. Pull the buns when they are a light golden brown and set aside.

1 Turn the griddle on to medium/high to high heat (above 400°F [200°C]).

2 Once the griddle is to temperature, lay the oil on the griddle.

3 Place the 2 meatballs in the oil, ensuring space between the meatballs to give them room to be smashed.

4 Sprinkle salt and pepper liberally onto the meatballs.

5 After about 30 seconds, place a handful of the thinly sliced onions onto each meatball and smash each meatball all the way down flat with a burger smasher or the back side of the spatula, using the back side of another spatula to help apply pressure. Hold the smash down for 10–15 seconds.

6 Once each burger is smashed and you see the juices begin to rise to the surface (almost immediately), use the spatula and quickly flip them and place a slice of American cheese on each burger.

7 Pull each burger from the heat. The cheese will continue to melt while building the burger.

8 Place the burgers, stacking one on top of the other, and place on the bottom bun. Dress the burger with your favorite toppings. Serve and enjoy!

The Molly Smash Burger

SERVINGS: 1 burger | **PREP TIME:** 10 minutes | **COOK TIME:** 4–6 minutes

Tommy Scarano of The Gallery Backyard BBQ makes this amazing sandwich and graciously allowed us to include it in this book. It's the brown sugar crust that sets this one apart.

2 tablespoons (30 g) brown sugar

7 ounces (200 g) 80/20 ground beef, divided into two 3½-ounce (100 g) loosely packed meatballs

1 tablespoon (14 g) unsalted butter

½ red onion, sliced

1 tablespoon (15 ml) vegetable oil

2 teaspoons salt (to taste)

2 teaspoons pepper (to taste)

2 teaspoons garlic powder

2 slices American cheese

1 hamburger bun

Note: You'll need parchment paper for this recipe.

1 Turn the griddle on to medium/high to high heat (above 400°F [200°C]).

2 Place the brown sugar in a small bowl or on a plate.

3 Roll each meatball in the brown sugar, getting as much of the meatball covered as possible.

4 Lay the butter on the griddle, followed by the onions. Cook until the onions begin to turn translucent (about 5–6 minutes) and move to the side of the griddle.

5 Once the griddle is to temperature, lay the oil on the griddle. Place the brown sugar-coated burger balls on the griddle and let sit for up to 20 seconds. Then, top each one with a piece of parchment paper. Press and hold for 13 seconds.

6 When your edges start to brown, flip and season with the salt, pepper, and garlic powder.

7 After 30 seconds, place a slice of American cheese on each burger.

8 Pull each burger from the heat. The cheese will continue to melt while building the burger.

9 Place the burgers, stacking one on top of the other, and place on the bottom bun. Top with a pile of the sautéed onions and place the top bun. Serve and enjoy!

Pizza Smash Burger

SERVINGS: 2 burgers | **PREP TIME:** 10 minutes | **COOK TIME:** 8–10 minutes

When the moon hits your eye with this Pizza Smash Burger, we don't think it'll be love, but maybe something more along the lines of infatuation.

4 slices garlic Texas toast

1 tablespoon (15 ml) vegetable oil

12 ounces (340 g)
80/20 ground beef, divided
into four 3-ounce (85 g) loosely
packed meatballs

2 teaspoons salt (to taste)

2 teaspoons pepper (to taste)

½ cup (60 g) shredded
mozzarella cheese

8 slices pepperoni

½ cup (123 g) pizza sauce

4 pepperoncini, diced

1. Turn the griddle on to medium/high to high heat (above 400°F [200°C]).

2. While the griddle is coming up to temperature, place the garlic Texas toast on the griddle. Cook until it is a light golden brown and then flip. Once the other side is toasted to a light golden brown, pull and set aside.

3. Once the griddle is to temperature, lay the oil on the griddle.

4. Place the 4 meatballs in the oil, ensuring space between the meatballs to give them room to be smashed.

5. Sprinkle salt and pepper liberally on the meatballs.

6. After about 30 seconds, smash each meatball all the way down flat with a burger smasher or the back side of the spatula, using the back side of another spatula to help apply pressure. Hold the smash down for 10–15 seconds.

7. Once each burger is smashed and you see the juices begin to rise to the surface (almost immediately), use the spatula and quickly flip them and place a handful of the shredded mozzarella cheese on each burger, followed by the pepperoni. It will help with placement if you place the slices of pepperoni directly on the griddle for about 30 seconds before placing on the burger.

8. Pull each burger from the heat. The cheese will continue to melt while building the burgers. Place the burgers, stacking one on top of each other, on the bottom slices of garlic Texas toast. Pour 1/4 cup (62g) of pizza sauce on each burger and top with the pepperoncini and the top slices of the garlic Texas toast. Serve and enjoy!

Our Classic WALTWINS Diner Smash Burger

SERVINGS: 1 burger | **PREP TIME:** 10 minutes | **COOK TIME:** 4 minutes

The name says it all. This is the burger that made us fall in love with the griddle. So simple, yet it's the best burger we've ever had. You could start a food truck or restaurant with this as your main menu item. In fact, we may just do that!

1 tablespoon (15 ml) vegetable oil

6–7 ounces (170 to 200 g) 80/20 ground beef, divided into 2 loose meatballs

2 teaspoons salt (to taste)

2 teaspoons pepper (to taste)

2 slices American cheese

1 potato hamburger bun

Ketchup, for topping

Mustard, for topping

Mayonnaise, for topping

4 dill pickle chips

Shredded lettuce, for topping

1 tomato, sliced

½ red onion, thinly sliced

OPTIONAL:
additional 1 tablespoon (14 g) mayonnaise, for toasting the buns

1 Turn the griddle on to medium/high to high heat (above 400°F [200°C]).

2 Once the griddle is to temperature, lay the oil on the griddle.

3 Place the 2 meatballs in the oil, ensuring space between the meatballs to give them room to be smashed.

4 Sprinkle salt and pepper liberally on the meatballs.

5 After about 30 seconds, smash each meatball all the way down flat with a burger smasher or the back side of the spatula, using the back side of another spatula to help apply pressure. Hold the smash down for 10–15 seconds.

6 Once each burger is smashed and you see the juices begin to rise to the surface (almost immediately), use the spatula and quickly flip them and place a slice of American cheese on each burger.

Note: The toppings we list are our preferences. Feel free to dress your burgers to your own liking. The Classic Smash Burger to us consists of ketchup, mustard, mayonnaise, pickles, shredded lettuce, sliced tomato, sliced onion, and of course, American cheese!

7 Pull each burger from the heat. The cheese will continue to melt while building the burger.

8 Place the burgers, stacking one on top of the other, on the bottom bun. Build in the following order (optional): bottom bun, swirl of ketchup, swirl of mustard, swirl of mayonnaise, pickle chips, smash burger patties, lettuce, tomato, onion, top bun. Serve and enjoy!

If toasting the buns: While the griddle is coming up to temperature, spread the mayonnaise on the inside of the top and bottom buns and lay them on the griddle facedown. Pull the buns when they are a light golden brown and set aside.

Surf 'n' Turf Smash Burger

SERVINGS: 1 burger | **PREP TIME:** 10 minutes | **COOK TIME:** 4 minutes

This smash burger became an instant WALTWINS favorite. This is one that goes in the "Don't knock it till you try it" category. When you impress the masses with this smash burger, they'll be convinced you went to culinary school. Note that while we do sometimes make our own Alfredo sauce from scratch, we have found that heated up store-bought jarred Alfredo sauce works great in a time crunch.

1 tablespoon (15 ml) vegetable oil

6–7 ounces (170 to 200 g) 80/20 ground beef, divided into 2 loose meatballs

2½ teaspoons salt, divided (to taste)

2½ teaspoons pepper, divided (to taste)

1 tablespoon (14 g) butter

1 tablespoon (6 g) minced garlic

¼ pound (115 g) small shrimp, peeled and deveined

½ cup (40 g) shredded Parmesan cheese, plus additional for topping

1 brioche-style hamburger bun

½ red onion, thinly sliced

½ cup (125 g) of your favorite Alfredo sauce, or homemade Alfredo sauce

OPTIONAL:
additional 1 tablespoon (14 g) mayonnaise, for toasting the buns

1 Turn the griddle on to medium/high to high heat (above 400°F [200°C]).

2 Once the griddle is to temperature, lay the oil on the griddle.

3 Place the 2 meatballs in the oil, ensuring space between the meatballs to give them room to be smashed.

4 Sprinkle salt and pepper liberally onto the meatballs.

5 After about 30 seconds, smash each meatball all the way down flat with a burger smasher or the back side of the spatula, using the back side of another spatula to help apply pressure. Hold the smash down for 10–15 seconds.

6 On the other side of the griddle, lay the butter and the garlic down. Once the butter is melted, place the shrimp on top. Add ½ teaspoon each of salt and pepper. After about 3 minutes, flip the shrimp, continue to cook until they turn pink, and then pull from the griddle.

7 Once each burger is smashed and you see the juices begin to rise to the surface (almost immediately), use the spatula and quickly flip them and place a handful of the shredded Parmesan cheese on each burger.

8 Pull each burger from the heat. The cheese will continue to melt while building the burger.

9 Place the burgers, stacking one on top of the other, on the bottom bun. Build in the following order: bottom bun, onion, smash burger patties, 3–4 pieces of shrimp, Alfredo sauce, more shredded Parmesan cheese, top bun. Serve and enjoy!

If toasting the buns: While the griddle is coming up to temperature, spread the mayonnaise on the inside of the top and bottom buns and lay them on the griddle facedown. Pull the buns when they are a light golden brown and set aside.

If toasting the buns: While the griddle is coming up to temperature, spread the mayonnaise on the inside of the top and bottom buns and lay them on the griddle facedown. Pull the buns when they are a light golden brown and set aside.

Smash Burger Royale

SERVINGS: 1 burger | **PREP TIME:** 10 minutes | **COOK TIME:** 4 minutes

If you ever wondered if an egg belongs on a burger, this one answers that question . . . yes, yes it does! It'll make you ask yourself why you haven't been doing this all along.

1 tablespoon (15 ml) vegetable oil

1 large egg

2½ teaspoons salt, divided (to taste)

2½ teaspoons pepper, divided (to taste)

6–7 ounces (170 to 200 g) 80/20 ground beef, divided into 2 loose meatballs

2 slices American cheese

1 potato hamburger bun

Ketchup, for topping

Mustard, for topping

Mayonnaise, for topping

4 dill pickle chips

Shredded lettuce, for topping

Sliced tomato, for topping

½ red onion, thinly sliced

OPTIONAL:
additional 1 tablespoon (14 g) mayonnaise, for toasting the buns

1 Turn the griddle on to medium/high to high heat (above 400°F [200°C]).

2 Once the griddle is to temperature, lay the oil on the griddle.

3 Crack the egg on the griddle surface and pour onto the griddle. Wait until the white is completely opaque to gently flip the egg, season with ½ teaspoon each of salt and pepper, and pull from the surface after 30 seconds to a minute, trying not to break the yolk.

4 Place the 2 meatballs in the oil, ensuring space between the meatballs to give them room to be smashed.

5 Sprinkle salt and pepper liberally onto the meatballs.

6 After about 30 seconds, smash each meatball all the way down flat with a burger smasher or the back side of the spatula, using the back side of another spatula to help apply pressure. Hold the smash down for 10–15 seconds.

7 Once each burger is smashed and you see the juices begin to rise to the surface (almost immediately), use the spatula and quickly flip them and place a slice of American cheese on each burger.

8 Pull each burger from the heat. The cheese will continue to melt while building the burger.

9 Place the burgers, stacking one on top of the other, on the bottom bun. Build in the following order (optional): bottom bun, swirl of ketchup, swirl of mustard, swirl of mayonnaise, pickle chips, smash burger patties, egg, lettuce, tomato, onion, top bun. Serve and enjoy!

Pastrami Melt Smash Burger

SERVINGS: 2 burgers | **PREP TIME:** 15 minutes | **COOK TIME:** 4 minutes

This is what you get when a New York Deli merges with your favorite Mom-and-Pop burger joint. It's business on top with the pastrami and all gooey goodness on the bottom with the melty cheese. You can also add a heaping spoonful of sauerkraut to make this a Reuben Smash Burger!

4 slices marbled rye bread

1 tablespoon (14 g) unsalted butter

1 tablespoon (15 ml) vegetable oil

12 ounces (340 g) 80/20 ground beef, divided into four 3-ounce (85 g) loosely packed meatballs

½ pound (225 g) deli sliced pastrami

4 slices Swiss cheese

Russian Dressing, for topping (See recipe page 33)

1 Turn the griddle on to medium/high to high heat (above 400°F [200°C]).

2 While the griddle is coming up to temperature, spread the butter on one side of each slice of bread and lay butter-side down on the griddle. Pull the bread when it is a light golden brown and set aside.

3 Once the griddle is to temperature, lay the oil on the griddle.

4 Place the 4 meatballs in the oil, ensuring space between the meatballs to give them room to be smashed.

5 After about 30 seconds, smash each meatball all the way down flat with a burger smasher or the back side of the spatula, using the back side of another spatula to help apply pressure. Hold the smash down for 10–15 seconds.

6 As the burgers begin to cook, lay the pastrami on the griddle to lightly brown each slice.

7 Once each burger is smashed and you see the juices begin to rise to the surface (almost immediately), use the spatula and quickly flip them and place a slice of Swiss cheese on each burger.

8 Pull the pastrami off the griddle and divide evenly, stacking the pastrami on top of each burger.

9 Pull each burger from the heat.

10 Place the pastrami burgers, stacking one on top of the other, on the bottom slices of bread. Spread a generous amount of Russian Dressing on the top slices of bread and place on top of the pastrami burgers. Serve and enjoy!

Russian Dressing

½ cup (115 g) mayonnaise
3 tablespoons (45 g) ketchup
2 tablespoons (30 g) horseradish
2 teaspoons Worcestershire sauce
1 tablespoon (13 g) sugar
¼ teaspoons paprika
1 medium dill pickle, diced
Salt and pepper (to taste)

Whisk all the ingredients together in a medium size bowl until the consistency is that of a thick dressing. Add salt and pepper to taste.

Smashed Pub Sliders

SERVINGS: 1 serving of 3 mini burgers | **PREP TIME:** 10 minutes | **COOK TIME:** 4 minutes

The Classic Pub Burger is smashed and made into smaller sliders.
What they may lack in size, they more than make up for in taste!

1 tablespoon (15 ml)
vegetable oil

6 ounces (170 g)
80/20 ground beef, divided into
three 2-ounce (55 g) loosely
packed meatballs

2 teaspoons salt (to taste)

2 teaspoons pepper (to taste)

3 slices American cheese

3 King's Hawaiian
Pretzel Slider Buns

Leafy lettuce, for topping

6 dill pickle chips, for topping

Red onion, thinly sliced,
for topping

Basic Cheese Sauce
(See recipe on page 36),
or your favorite cheese sauce,
for topping

Optional: 1 tablespoon
(14 g) mayonnaise, for
toasting the buns

1   Turn the griddle on to medium/high to high heat (above 400°F [200°C]).

2   Once the griddle is to temperature, lay the oil on the griddle.

3   Place the 3 meatballs in the oil, ensuring space between the meatballs to give them room to be smashed.

4   Sprinkle salt and pepper liberally onto the meatballs.

5   After about 30 seconds, smash each meatball all the way down flat with a burger smasher or the back side of the spatula, using the back side of another spatula to help apply pressure. Hold the smash down for 10–15 seconds.

6   Once each burger is smashed and you see the juices begin to rise to the surface (almost immediately), use the spatula and quickly flip them and place a slice of American cheese on each burger.

7   Pull each burger from the heat. The cheese will continue to melt while building the burgers.

8   Place the burgers on the bottom buns. Build in the following order: bottom bun, lettuce, smash burger patties, pickle chips, onion, Basic Cheese Sauce, top bun. Serve and enjoy!

Basic Cheese Sauce

2 tablespoons (28 g) butter
2 tablespoons (16 g) all-purpose flour
2 cups (475 ml) milk
2 cups (225 g) shredded cheddar cheese
1–2 teaspoons salt (to taste)
1–2 cups (113 to 226 g) shredded
   American cheese (to taste)

1 On the stove or on the griddle over medium/high heat (375 to 400°F [190 to 200°C]), place the butter in a medium saucepan.

2 Once the butter is melted, stir in the flour to create a roux.

3 As soon as the flour is thoroughly mixed in, begin pouring in the milk, a little at a time. As the roux and milk thicken, add more milk. Repeat until all the milk has been added.

4 Next, add in the shredded cheddar cheese and mix until the cheese is completely melted. Begin adding the salt and shredded American cheese. Start with 1 teaspoon of salt and 1 cup (113 g) of American cheese and add both to your desired taste.

5 Serve and enjoy!

Note: The cheese sauce will begin to solidify when it cools down. Simply reheat to a liquid consistency when ready to use.

It's All in Your Bread

Use your favorite buns! We've tasted and tested just about every roll and bun you can think of, and we've come to love—and been able to rely on—potato buns. And although we've made recommendations throughout this book, we encourage you to use your imagination, make the most of every smash burger experience, and swap in the bun or roll that will make you and your guests happiest.

But if you're looking for more inspiration, we also love Hawaiian rolls (for sliders!), brioche buns, and your everyday sesame seed buns.

The breads we recommend for paninis vary depending on the cook, and you'll see our suggestions in chapter 3. But some of our go-to choices for paninis and pressed sandwiches include sourdough, marbled rye, white mountain bread, and Texas toast. Remember, unless the cook calls for a specific bread, use your favorite!

Steak House Smash Burger

SERVINGS: 1 burger | **PREP TIME:** 10 minutes | **COOK TIME:** 4–6 minutes

Here, the humble smash burger takes on the lavish steak house. This smash burger is definitely a knockout, with sautéed mushrooms and onions doused in a savory steak sauce. It's fancy and messy all at once.

1 tablespoon (14 g) unsalted butter

½ small yellow onion, cut into ¼-inch (3 mm) slices

½ cup (35 g) white or baby bella mushrooms, sliced

1 tablespoon (15 ml) vegetable oil

6–7 ounces (170 to 200 g) 80/20 ground beef, divided into two 3- to 3½-ounce (85 to 100 g) loosely packed meatballs

2 teaspoons salt (to taste)

2 teaspoons pepper (to taste)

2 slices Swiss cheese

1 potato hamburger bun

2 tablespoons (30 g) steak sauce

OPTIONAL:
1 tablespoon (14 g) mayonnaise, for toasting the buns

1 Turn one side of the griddle on to medium/high to high heat (above 400°F [200°C]).

2 Turn the other side on to medium/low heat (300 to 325°F [150°C to 170°C]).

3 Once the medium/low side of the griddle is to temperature, lay the butter on the griddle. As the butter melts, place the onions and mushrooms down in the butter to begin cooking the vegetables. Continue cooking while preparing the burgers.

4 Once the medium/high to high side of the griddle is to temperature, lay the oil on the griddle.

5 Place the 2 meatballs in the oil, ensuring space between the meatballs to give them room to be smashed.

6 Sprinkle salt and pepper liberally on the meatballs.

7 After about 30 seconds, smash each meatball all the way down flat with a burger smasher or the back side of the spatula, using the back side of another spatula to help apply pressure. Hold the smash down for 10–15 seconds.

8 Once each burger is smashed and you see the juices begin to rise to the surface (almost immediately), use the spatula and quickly flip them and place a slice of Swiss cheese on each burger.

9 Pull each burger from the heat. The cheese will continue to melt while building the burger.

10 Once the mushrooms and onions are cooked, place the burgers, stacking one on top of the other, on the bottom bun. Lay the mushrooms and onions on the top burger. Pour the steak sauce over top and place on the top bun. Serve and enjoy!

Taco Smash Burger

SERVINGS: 2 burgers | **PREP TIME:** 10 minutes | **COOK TIME:** 4 minutes

When your family wants smash burgers, but it's "Taco Tuesday," this recipe will make everyone happy. It sure makes us happy!

1 tablespoon (15 ml) vegetable oil

12 ounces (340 g) 80/20 ground beef, divided into four 3-ounce (85 g) loosely packed meatballs

1 packet (1 ounce, or 28 g) taco seasoning

1 cup (225 g) shredded Mexican cheese blend

2 hamburger buns (We prefer potato buns.)

1 tomato, sliced

1 cup (43 g) shredded lettuce

½ cup (124 g) nacho cheese sauce

2 tablespoons (28 ml) taco sauce

1 Turn the griddle on to medium/high heat (375 to 400°F [190 to 200°C]).

2 Once the griddle is to temperature, lay the oil on the griddle.

3 Place the 4 meatballs in the oil, ensuring space between the meatballs to give them room to be smashed.

4 Sprinkle the taco seasoning liberally on the meatballs.

5 After about 30 seconds, smash each meatball all the way down flat with a burger smasher or the back side of the spatula, using the back side of another spatula to help apply pressure. Hold the smash down for 10–15 seconds.

6 Once each burger is smashed and you see the juices begin to rise to the surface (almost immediately), use the spatula and quickly flip them and place a handful of shredded Mexican cheese on each burger.

7 Pull each burger from the heat. The cheese will continue to melt while building the burgers.

8 Place the burgers, stacking one on top of the other, on the bottom buns. Build in the following order: bottom bun, smash burger patties, tomato, lettuce, nacho cheese sauce, taco sauce, top bun. Serve and enjoy!

Mushroom & Swiss Smash Burger

SERVINGS: 1 burger | **PREP TIME:** 10 minutes | **COOK TIME:** 6-8 minutes

The Mushroom & Swiss Smash Burger is one we lovingly refer to as a "game-changer." Once we learned this simple and decadent recipe, it became an instant classic—not just for us, but for our families as well!

1 tablespoon (15 ml) vegetable oil

6–7 ounces (170 to 200 g) 80/20 ground beef, divided into two 3- to 3½-ounce (85 to 100 g) loosely packed meatballs

2 teaspoons salt (to taste)

2 teaspoons pepper (to taste)

2 slices Swiss cheese

1 potato hamburger bun

Mushroom Gravy (See recipe on page 44)

OPTIONAL:
1 tablespoon (14 g) mayonnaise, for toasting the buns

1 Turn the griddle on to medium/high to high heat (above 400°F [200°C]).

2 Once the griddle is to temperature, lay the oil on the griddle.

3 Place the 2 meatballs in the oil, ensuring space between the meatballs to give them room to be smashed.

4 Sprinkle salt and pepper liberally on the meatballs.

5 After about 30 seconds, smash each meatball all the way down flat with a burger smasher or the back side of the spatula, using the back side of another spatula to help apply pressure. Hold the smash down for 10–15 seconds.

6 Once each burger is smashed and you see the juices begin to rise to the surface (almost immediately), use the spatula and quickly flip them and place a slice of Swiss cheese on each burger.

7 Pull each burger from the heat. The cheese will continue to melt while building the burger.

8 Place the burgers, stacking one on top of the other, on the bottom bun. Top with a generous spoonful of the Mushroom Gravy and place the top bun. Serve and enjoy!

Mushroom Gravy

4 tablespoons (55 g) butter, separated
2 tablespoons (16 g) all-purpose flour
2 cups (475 ml) beef stock, or beef broth
3 cups (210 g) sliced baby bella mushrooms
½ teaspoon salt
¼ teaspoon pepper
½ teaspoon Worcestershire Sauce
½ teaspoon soy sauce

1   In a medium saucepan over medium heat (350°F [180°C]) on the griddle, melt 2 tablespoons (28 g) of butter and slowly add the flour, mixing until a paste is created. Slowly stir in the beef stock or broth.

2   While the gravy is cooking and thickening, lay 2 more tablespoons (28 g) of butter on the griddle over medium/low heat (300 to 325°F [150°C to 170°C]), place the mushrooms in the butter, and add the salt and pepper.

3   While the mushrooms are sautéing, add Worcestershire sauce and soy sauce to the gravy. Once the mushrooms are softened, pull from the heat.

4   As the gravy comes to a boil, lower the heat and add the mushrooms.

5   Continue cooking for 4–5 minutes or until the sauce is thickened.

Asian-Inspired Smash Burger

SERVINGS: 1 burger | **PREP TIME:** 10 minutes | **COOK TIME:** 4 minutes

Adam's mother-in-law introduced us to ABC Sweet Soy Sauce, and we knew its sweet and savory flavor would pair perfectly with Asian-style coleslaw, 80/20 ground beef, and a sesame seed bun. We were right!

1 sesame seed hamburger bun

1 tablespoon (15 ml) vegetable oil

8 ounces (225 g) 80/20 ground beef mixture, divided into two 4-ounce (115 g) loosely packed meatballs

1 teaspoon minced ginger

2 teaspoons (12 g) minced garlic

½ tablespoon diced green onion

2 teaspoons salt, divided

1½ teaspoons pepper, divided

½ cup (120 ml) ABC Sweet Soy Sauce

½ cup (34 g) Asian-style coleslaw mix

Sweet Soy Burger Sauce, for topping (See recipe on page 47.)

1 Turn the griddle on to medium/high heat (375 to 400°F [190 to 200°C]).

2 While the griddle is coming up to temperature, place the buns on the griddle facedown to toast. Once they are golden brown, pull and set aside.

3 Mix the ground beef with the ginger, garlic, green onion, 1 teaspoon of salt, and ½ teaspoon of pepper until evenly distributed. Divide the mixture into 2 loosely packed meatballs.

4 Once the griddle is to temperature, lay the oil on the griddle.

5 Place the 2 meatballs in the oil, ensuring space between the meatballs to give them room to be smashed.

6 Sprinkle salt and pepper liberally on the meatballs.

7 After about 30 seconds, smash each meatball all the way down flat with a burger smasher or the back side of the spatula, using the back side of another spatula to help apply pressure. Hold the smash down for 10–15 seconds.

8 Pour ½ tablespoon of ABC Sweet Soy Sauce on each burger.

9 Once each burger is smashed and you see the juices begin to rise to the surface (almost immediately), use the spatula and quickly flip them. **CONTINUED ➜**

10 Pour another ½ tablespoon of ABC Sweet Soy Sauce on each burger.

11 After another minute, pull each burger from the heat.

12 Place the burgers, stacking one on top of the other, on the bottom bun, followed by the Asian-style coleslaw mix. Pour another ½ tablespoon of ABC Sweet Soy Sauce over the burger and coleslaw mix. Spread the Sweet Soy Burger Sauce on the inside of the top bun and place on top of the burger. Serve and enjoy!

Sweet Soy Burger Sauce

2 tablespoons (28 g) Kewpie mayonnaise, or your favorite brand of mayonnaise
3 tablespoons (45 ml) ABC Sweet Soy Sauce

Mix the mayonnaise and ABC Sweet Soy Sauce together and set aside.

Hawaiian Pineapple Smash Burger

SERVINGS: 1 burger | **PREP TIME:** 10 minutes | **COOK TIME:** 4 minutes

It may not be from the Islands, but with its perfect balance of savory and sweet, this crowd-pleasing burger will be a regular for your griddle. We promise!

1 recipe Teriyaki Sauce (See recipe on page 49.)

2 pineapple slices

1 tablespoon (14 g) mayonnaise

1 sesame seed hamburger bun

2 teaspoons salt (to taste)

2 teaspoons pepper (to taste)

1 tablespoon (15 ml) vegetable oil

6 ounces (170 g) 80/20 ground beef, divided into two 3-ounce (85 g) loosely packed meatballs

2 slices Swiss cheese

1 tomato, sliced

½ cup (22 g) shredded lettuce

1 Place the ground beef and ⅓ of the Teriyaki Sauce in a resealable plastic bag. Add the pineapple slices to a separate resealable plastic bag with another ⅓ of the marinade. Refrigerate for at least 2 hours. Set the last ⅓ of the marinade aside in a separate container to use as additional sauce for the burger.

2 Turn the griddle on to medium heat (350°F [180°C]).

3 While the griddle is coming up to temperature, spread the mayonnaise on the inside of the top and bottom buns and place on the griddle face-down. Pull the buns when they are a light golden brown and set aside.

4 Once the griddle is to temperature, lay the oil on the griddle. Place the 2 meatballs in the oil, ensuring space between the meatballs to give them room to be smashed.

5 Sprinkle salt and pepper liberally on the meatballs.

6 After about 30 seconds, smash each meatball all the way down flat with a burger smasher or the back side of the spatula, using the back side of another spatula to help apply pressure. Hold the smash down for 10–15 seconds.

7 Once each burger is smashed and you see the juices begin to rise to the surface (almost immediately), use a spatula and quickly flip them and place a slice of Swiss cheese on each burger.

8 Pull each burger from the heat and set aside. The cheese will continue to melt while building the burger.

Teriyaki Sauce

1¾ cups (410 ml) water
1 cup (235 ml) soy sauce
1 cup (225 g) brown sugar
½ teaspoon onion powder
½ teaspoon garlic powder

9 Place the marinated pineapple slices on the griddle surface. Cook on each side for 2 minutes.

10 Place the burgers, stacking one on top of the other, on the bottom bun. Build in the following order: bottom bun, smash burger patties, pineapple, tomatoes, lettuce, a drizzle of Teriyaki Sauce, top bun. Serve and enjoy!

1 Mix all the ingredients in a small saucepan over medium heat.

2 Bring the mixture to a boil and reduce the heat to simmer for 10 minutes.

3 Remove from the heat and let cool.

Texas BBQ Smash Burger

SERVINGS: 2 burgers | **PREP TIME:** 10 minutes | **COOK TIME:** 4 minutes

If you aren't from Texas, it won't matter because you'll fully understand the sentiment behind the saying "Don't mess with Texas!"

2 tablespoons (28 g) unsalted butter

4 slices Texas toast bread

1 tablespoon (15 ml) vegetable oil

12 ounces (340 g) 80/20 ground beef, divided into four 3-ounce (85 g) loosely packed meatballs

2 teaspoons salt (to taste)

2 teaspoons pepper (to taste)

4 slices Monterey Jack cheese, or cheese of your choice

1 tablespoon (14 g) mayonnaise

4 large fried onion rings

Texas-style BBQ sauce, for topping

1 Turn the griddle on to medium/high to high heat (above 400°F [200°C]).

2 While the griddle is coming up to temperature, spread butter on both sides of each slice of the Texas toast bread and place on the griddle. cook until it is a light golden brown and then flip. Once the other side is a light golden brown, pull and set aside.

3 Once the griddle is to temperature, lay the oil on the griddle.

4 Place the 4 meatballs in the oil, ensuring space between the meatballs to give them room to be smashed. Sprinkle salt and pepper liberally on the meatballs.

5 After about 30 seconds, smash each meatball all the way down flat with a burger smasher or the back side of the spatula, using the back side of another spatula to help apply pressure. Hold the smash down for 10–15 seconds.

6 Once each burger is smashed and you see the juices begin to rise to the surface (almost immediately), use the spatula and quickly flip them and place a slice of Monterey Jack cheese on each burger.

7 Pull each burger from the heat. The cheese will continue to melt while building the burgers.

8 Place the burgers, stacking one on top of the other, on the bottom slices of Texas toast. Build in the following order: bottom bread, spread of mayonnaise, smash burger patties, onion rings, Texas BBQ sauce. Add a spread of mayonnaise on the inside of the top slice of Texas toast and place on top of the burger. Serve and enjoy!

California Smash Burger with Avocado, Bacon, and Ranch

SERVINGS: 1 burger | **PREP TIME:** 10 minutes | **COOK TIME:** 4 minutes

With family ties to California, this burger pays homage to our parents' original stomping grounds. Our mom loved her avocado, bacon, and ranch with just about anything, and we know she'd agree that this one is incredible!

1 tablespoon (15 ml) vegetable oil

6–7 ounces (170 to 200 g) 80/20 ground beef, divided into two 3- to 3½-ounce (85 to 100 g) loosely packed meatballs

2 teaspoons salt (to taste)

2 teaspoons pepper (to taste)

2 slices Swiss cheese

1 potato hamburger bun

½ tablespoon mayonnaise

2 slices cooked bacon

2 tomato slices

1 small avocado, thinly sliced

½ red onion, thinly sliced

Ranch dressing, for topping

OPTIONAL:
additional 1 tablespoon (14 g) mayonnaise, for toasting the buns

1 Turn the griddle on to medium/high to high heat (above 400°F [200°C]).

2 Once the griddle is to temperature, lay the oil on the griddle.

3 Place the 2 meatballs in the oil, ensuring space between the meatballs to give them room to be smashed. Sprinkle salt and pepper liberally on the meatballs.

4 After about 30 seconds, smash each meatball all the way down flat with a burger smasher or the back side of the spatula, using the back side of another spatula to help apply pressure. Hold the smash down for 10–15 seconds.

5 Once each burger is smashed and you see the juices begin to rise to the surface (almost immediately), use the spatula and quickly flip them and place a slice of Swiss cheese on each burger.

6 Pull each burger from the heat. The cheese will continue to melt while building the burger.

7 Place the burgers, stacking one on top of the other, on the bottom bun. Build in the following order: bottom bun, mayonnaise, smash burger patties, bacon, tomatoes, avocado, additional pinch of salt and pepper, onion, ranch dressing. Add another spread of mayonnaise on the top bun and place on top of the burger. Serve and enjoy!

If toasting the buns: While the griddle is coming up to temperature, spread the mayonnaise on the inside of the top and bottom buns and lay them on the griddle facedown. Pull the buns when they are a light golden brown and set aside.

Chili Cheese Smash Burger

SERVINGS: 1 burger | **PREP TIME:** 10 minute | **COOK TIME:** 4 minutes

While chili may be associated with fall and winter seasons, to be able to enjoy it all year long, may we suggest placing your chili of choice on a cheesed smash burger? Boom! Meet your new year-round pick.

1 tablespoon (15 ml) vegetable oil

6 ounces (170 g) 80/20 ground beef, divided into two 3-ounce (85 g) loosely packed meatballs

2 teaspoons salt (to taste)

2 teaspoons pepper (to taste)

2 slices American cheese

1 potato hamburger bun

½ cup (124 g) chili, heated

½ cup (58 g) shredded cheddar cheese

½ red onion, thinly sliced

1 Turn the griddle on to medium/high to high heat (above 400°F [200°C]).

2 Once the griddle is to temperature, lay the oil on the griddle.

3 Place the 2 meatballs in the oil, ensuring space between the meatballs to give them room to be smashed.

4 Sprinkle salt and pepper liberally on the meatballs.

5 After about 30 seconds, smash each meatball all the way down flat with a burger smasher or the back side of the spatula, using the back side of another spatula to help apply pressure. Hold the smash down for 10–15 seconds.

6 Once each burger is smashed and you see the juices begin to rise to the surface (almost immediately), use the spatula and quickly flip them and place a slice of America cheese on each burger.

7 Pull each burger from the heat. The cheese will continue to melt while building the burger.

8 Place the burgers, stacking one on top of the other, on the bottom bun. Place the chili on top of the burger, followed by the shredded cheddar cheese and onion. Place the top bun on the burger. Serve and enjoy!

French Dip Smash Burger

SERVINGS: 1 burger | **PREP TIME:** 10 minutes | **COOK TIME:** 4 minutes

Have you ever had a burger at a joint that you can still think about and remember exactly how it made you feel the first time you tried it? We introduce to you the French Dip Smash Burger. It's your next great burger joint experience, but from the luxury of your own backyard.

1 tablespoon (15 ml) vegetable oil

6 ounces (170 g) 80/20 ground beef, divided into two 3-ounce (85 g) loosely packed meatballs

2 teaspoons salt (to taste)

2 teaspoons pepper (to taste)

2 slices Swiss cheese

1 potato hamburger bun

4 ounces (115 g) leftover roast beef, or deli sliced roast beef

½ white onion, thinly sliced

1 packet (1 ounce, or 28 g) au jus gravy mix, prepared

1   Turn the griddle on to medium/high to high heat (above 400°F [200°C]).

2   Once the griddle is to temperature, lay the oil on the griddle.

3   Place the 2 meatballs in the oil, ensuring space between the meatballs to give them room to be smashed. Sprinkle salt and pepper liberally on the meatballs.

4   After about 30 seconds, smash each meatball all the way down flat with a burger smasher or the back side of the spatula, using the back side of another spatula to help apply pressure. Hold the smash down for 10–15 seconds.

5   Once each burger is smashed and you see the juices begin to rise to the surface (almost immediately), use the spatula and quickly flip them and place a slice of Swiss cheese on each burger.

6   Pull each burger from the heat. The cheese will continue to melt while building the burger.

7   Place the burgers, stacking one on top of the other, on the bottom bun.

8   Place the roast beef onto the griddle to heat up. After about 30 seconds, flip and let heat for an additional 15 seconds and pull.

9   Place the roast beef on top of the burgers and place onions on top. Pour 1 tablespoon (15 ml) of the au jus over the beef and onions and place the top bun. Keep a small cup of the au jus close by to dip the burger in before each bite. Serve and enjoy!

Onion Soup Mix Smash Burger

SERVINGS: 1 burger | **PREP TIME:** 10 minutes | **COOK TIME:** 4 minutes

Do you remember when mom or grandma would make burgers at home, and you just couldn't put your finger on why it was so dang good? We're pretty sure it's this "secret" ingredient: onion soup mix.

1 ounce (28 g) onion soup mix, approximately ½ packet (We use Lipton Recipe Secrets Onion Soup & Dip Mix.)

6–7 ounces (170 to 200 g) 80/20 ground beef

1 tablespoon (15 ml) vegetable oil

2 teaspoons salt (to taste)

2 teaspoons pepper (to taste)

2 slices provolone cheese

1 potato hamburger bun

Ketchup, for topping

Mustard, for topping

Mayonnaise, for topping

4 dill pickle chips

½ red onion, thinly sliced

1 tomato, sliced

OPTIONAL:
additional 1 tablespoon (14 g) mayonnaise, for toasting the buns

1 Before cooking, take the onion soup mix and fold into the ground beef.

2 Divide the ground beef mixture into two evenly sized loosely packed meatballs.

3 Turn the griddle on to medium/high to high heat (above 400°F [200°C]).

4 Once the griddle is to temperature, lay the oil on the griddle.

5 Place the 2 meatballs in the oil, ensuring space between the meatballs to give them room to be smashed. Sprinkle salt and pepper liberally on the meatballs.

6 After about 30 seconds, smash each meatball all the way down flat with a burger smasher or the back side of the spatula, using the back side of another spatula to help apply pressure. Hold the smash down for 10–15 seconds.

7 Once each burger is smashed and you see the juices begin to rise to the surface (almost immediately), use the spatula and quickly flip them and place a slice of provolone cheese on each burger.

8 Pull each burger from the heat. The cheese will continue to melt while building the burger.

9 Place the burgers, stacking one on top of the other, on the bottom bun. Build in the following order (optional): bottom bun, swirl of ketchup, swirl of mustard, swirl of mayonnaise, pickle chips, smash burger patties, onion, tomato, top bun. Serve and enjoy!

Italian Smash Burger

SERVINGS: 2 burgers | **PREP TIME:** 10 minutes | **COOK TIME:** 4 minutes

This incredible recipe was gifted to us by Steve Bremer. This is why we love doing what we do—sharing the joy and love of cooking! Thank you, Steve!

¼ teaspoon baking soda

12 ounces (340 g) 80/20 ground beef

3 tablespoons (36 g) Freddy's Steakhouse Famous Steakburger and Fry Seasoning

½ small white onion, minced

4–6 pepperoncini

1 tablespoon (14 g) butter

2 potato hamburger buns

Garlic salt, for sprinkling on buns

1 tablespoon (15 ml) vegetable oil

1 teaspoon salt (to taste)

1 teaspoon pepper (to taste)

½ cup (60 g) shredded mozzarella cheese

½ cup (122 g) pizza sauce

1 Mix the baking soda with the ground beef. Sprinkle in the Freddy's Seasoning and let the mixture sit for approximately 15 minutes. The baking soda helps the ground beef to retain moisture.

2 Mince the onions and pepperoncini together.

3 Turn the griddle on to medium/high to high heat (above 400°F [200°C]).

4 While the griddle is coming up to temperature, spread the butter on the inside of the top and bottom buns, sprinkle with garlic salt, and lay them on the griddle facedown. Pull the buns when they are a light golden brown and set aside.

5 Once the griddle is to temperature, lay the oil on the griddle.

6 Place the 4 meatballs in the oil, ensuring space between the meatballs to give them room to be smashed.

7 Sprinkle salt and pepper liberally on the meatballs.

If toasting the buns: While the griddle is coming up to temperature, spread the mayonnaise on the inside of the top and bottom buns and lay them on the griddle facedown. Pull the buns when they are a light golden brown and set aside.

8 After about 30 seconds, smash each meatball all the way down flat with a burger smasher or the back side of the spatula, using the backside of another spatula to help apply pressure. Hold the smash down for 10–15 seconds.

9 Once each burger is smashed and you see the juices begin to rise to the surface (almost immediately), use the spatula and quickly flip them and place the shredded mozzarella cheese on each burger.

10 Pull each burger from the heat. The cheese will continue to melt while building the burgers.

11 Place the burgers, stacking one on top of the other, on the bottom bun. Place the minced onions and pepperoncini on the burgers. Spread the pizza sauce on the top buns and place on top of the burgers. Serve and enjoy!

Green Hatch Chile Smash Burger

SERVINGS: 1 burger | **PREP TIME:** 10 minutes | **COOK TIME:** 10-12 minutes (20 minutes if including bacon as part of the cook)

Here's a shout-out to our New Mexico PEEPS! This was a burger that was heavily requested of us. When we finally got around to doing our version (a Whataburger copycat), we understood why there were so many people calling for us to do this one. It was so we could know what they already knew—it's incredible!

4 slices thick cut bacon

1 tablespoon (15 ml) vegetable oil

8 ounces (225 g) 80/20 ground beef, divided into two 3- to 3½-ounce (85 to 100 g) loosely packed meatballs

2 teaspoons salt (to taste)

2 teaspoons pepper (to taste)

2 slices American cheese

2 slices Monterey Jack cheese

1 potato hamburger bun

Mayonnaise, for topping

1 can (4 ounces, or 115 g) Hatch green chiles

OPTIONAL:
additional 1 tablespoon (14 g) mayonnaise, for toasting the buns

Note: Here's a pro tip—heat the chiles on the griddle for 10-15 seconds before placing on the burgers.

Cook the bacon:

1 Turn the griddle on to medium heat (350°F [180°C]).

2 While the griddle is warming, place the strips of bacon on the griddle. (We have found that placing the bacon on the griddle before it is hot helps keep the bacon from curling too much.)

3 Cook the first side until browned and flip.

4 Continue to cook until the bacon is done to the desired crispiness. Pull and place on a paper towel–lined plate to drain off excess grease.

Cook the burgers:

1 Once the griddle is to temperature, lay the oil on the griddle.

2 Place the 2 meatballs in the oil, ensuring space between the meatballs to give them room to be smashed.

3 Sprinkle salt and pepper liberally on the meatballs.

4 After about 30 seconds, smash each meatball all the way down flat with a burger smasher or the back side of the spatula, using the back side of another spatula to help apply pressure. Hold the smash down for 10-15 seconds.

5 Once each burger is smashed and you see the juices begin to rise to the surface (almost immediately), use the spatula and quickly flip them and place the slices of cheese on each burger (2 slices of American on one and 2 slices of Monterey Jack on the other).

6 Pull each burger from the heat. The cheese will continue to melt while building the burger.

7 Place the burgers, stacking one on top of the other, on the bottom bun. Build in the following order: bottom bun, spread of mayonnaise, smash burger patties, 2 slices of bacon, crisscrossed on the burger, a heap of Hatch green chiles. Spread mayonnaise on the inside of the top bun and place on top of the burger. Serve and enjoy!

Lettuce "Wrapped" Smash Burger

SERVINGS: 1 burger | **PREP TIME:** 10 minutes | **COOK TIME:** 4 minutes

Cutting back on carbs? We got you! The same unbelievable smash burger flavor can be had with this "healthier" option. Managing the lettuce wrap may be a little messy, but it's so worth it!

1 tablespoon (15 ml) vegetable oil

6–7 ounces (170 to 200 g) 80/20 ground beef, divided into two 3- to 3½-ounce (85 to 100 g) loosely packed meatballs

2 teaspoons salt (to taste)

2 teaspoons pepper (to taste)

2 slices American cheese

4 large iceberg lettuce leaves

Ketchup, for topping

Mustard, for topping

Mayonnaise, for topping

4 dill pickle chips

½ red onion, thinly sliced

1 tomato, sliced

1 Turn the griddle on to medium/high to high heat (above 400°F [200°C]).

2 Once the griddle is to temperature, lay the oil on the griddle.

3 Place the 2 meatballs in the oil, ensuring space between the meatballs to give them room to be smashed.

4 Sprinkle salt and pepper liberally on the meatballs.

5 After about 30 seconds, smash each meatball all the way down flat with a burger smasher or the back side of the spatula, using the back side of another spatula to help apply pressure. Hold the smash down for 10–15 seconds.

6 Once each burger is smashed and you see the juices begin to rise to the surface (almost immediately), use the spatula and quickly flip them, and place a slice of American cheese on each burger.

7 Pull each burger from the heat. The cheese will continue to melt while building the burger.

8 Place the burgers, stacking one on top of the other, in the lettuce leaves. Build in the following order (optional): swirl of ketchup, swirl of mustard, swirl of mayonnaise, pickle chips, onion, tomato. Wrap the lettuce around the loaded burger. Eat it while it's hot, as the lettuce will quickly begin to wilt! Enjoy!

Cheese Skirt Smash Burger

SERVINGS: 1 burger | **PREP TIME:** 10 minutes | **COOK TIME:** 4 minutes

This cook was inspired by a California joint called the "Squeeze Inn." Brett decided we had to try it for ourselves on the griddle. This smash burger is all decked out in a yummy cheese "skirt," a large circle of crispy melted cheese surrounding the burger. How fancy!

1 tablespoon (15 ml) vegetable oil

6–7 ounces (170 to 200 g) 80/20 ground beef, divided into two 3- to 3½-ounce (85 to 100 g) loosely packed meatballs

2 teaspoons salt (to taste)

2 teaspoons pepper (to taste)

1 cup (115 g) shredded cheddar cheese

1 potato hamburger bun

Ketchup, for topping

Mustard, for topping

Mayonnaise, for topping

4 dill pickle chips

Shredded lettuce, for topping

1 tomato, sliced

½ red onion, thinly sliced

OPTIONAL:
additional 1 tablespoon (14 g) mayonnaise, for toasting the buns

1 Turn the griddle on to medium/high to high heat (above 400°F [200°C]).

2 Once the griddle is to temperature, lay the oil on the griddle.

3 Place the 2 meatballs in the oil, ensuring space between the meatballs to give them room to be smashed.

4 Sprinkle salt and pepper liberally on the meatballs.

5 After about 30 seconds, smash each meatball all the way down flat with a burger smasher or the back side of the spatula, using the back side of another spatula to help apply pressure. Hold the smash down for 10–15 seconds.

6 Once each burger is smashed and you see the juices begin to rise to the surface (almost immediately), use the spatula and quickly flip them and place a large handful of shredded cheddar cheese on one of the burgers, ensuring that a large area surrounding the burger is also covered in cheese.

7 Place the top bun directly on the burger and cover with a dome to ensure that the cheese melts.

8 Once the cheese is melted, pull and place on the second burger.

9 Dress the bottom bun in the following order (optional): swirl of ketchup, swirl of mustard, swirl of mayonnaise, pickle chips, lettuce, tomato, and onion. Place the smash burger patties, with the cheese overlapping, on the toppings and place the top bun. Serve and enjoy!

Donut Smash Burger

SERVINGS: 1 burger | **PREP TIME:** 10 minutes | **COOK TIME:** 4 minutes (20 minutes if including bacon as part of the cook)

With the perfect balance of savory and sweet, we jokingly call this the "Hannah Montana" burger because it is absolutely the "Best of Both Worlds!" You know . . . like the theme song from the Disney Channel show *Hannah Montana*, way back in 2006, remember?

2 slices bacon

1 tablespoon (15 ml) vegetable oil

6–7 ounces (170 to 200 g) 80/20 ground beef, divided into two 3- to 3½-ounce (85 to 100 g) loosely packed meatballs

2 teaspoons salt (to taste)

2 teaspoons pepper (to taste)

2 slices American cheese

2 glazed donuts

Note: This is wild and crazy as is, but feel free to go nuts with toppings of your choice!

Cook the bacon:

1 Turn the griddle on to medium heat (350°F [180°C]).

2 While the griddle is warming, place the strips of bacon on the griddle. (We have found that placing the bacon on the griddle before it is hot helps keep the bacon from curling too much.)

3 Cook the first side until browned and flip.

4 Continue to cook until the bacon is done to the desired crispiness. Pull and place on a paper towel–lined plate to drain off excess grease.

Cook the burger:

1 Turn the griddle on to medium/high to high heat (above 400°F [200°C]).

2 Once the griddle is to temperature, lay the oil on the griddle.

3 Place the 2 meatballs in the oil, ensuring space between the meatballs to give them room to be smashed.

4 Sprinkle salt and pepper liberally on the meatballs.

5 After about 30 seconds, smash each meatball all the way down flat with a burger smasher or the back side of the spatula, using the back side of another spatula to help apply pressure. Hold the smash down for 10–15 seconds.

6 Once each burger is smashed and you see the juices begin to rise to the surface (almost immediately), use the spatula and quickly flip them and place a slice of American cheese on each burger.

7 Pull each burger from the heat. The cheese will continue to melt while building the burger.

8 Place the burgers, stacking one on top of the other, and place on one of the donuts. Place the other donut on top. Serve and enjoy!

Advice for Griddle Clean-up

IF YOU HAVE A COLD-ROLLED STEEL GRIDDLE:
- Scrape any excess food (as much as you can).
- With the griddle on low, squirt water on the surface to loosen any stuck-on foods. Scrape the foods away, and wipe with a towel/paper towel.
- Once it is free of food and feels relatively smooth, pour a thin layer of oil on the griddle, and spread it evenly across the griddle with the towel.
- If the towel still appears dirty after this step, repeat the oil and wipe. Sometimes it will take an additional two or three times until the towel looks clean.

TOR A CERAMIC TOP GRIDDLE, same process through scraping the food after using the squirt bottle and scraping. From there, use hot water and soap, along with a scrub sponge, and wipe/scrub the surface with the soapy water. Rinse the griddle surface with clean water, and dry the griddle once sufficiently cleaned.

Disclaimer: It is always best to follow the manufacturer's recommendations for maintenance and cleaning.

The Quad D: Daddy Dutch Double Deluxe

SERVINGS: 2 burgers | **PREP TIME:** 10 minutes | **COOK TIME:** 4 minutes

Our great friend Kent, a.k.a. Daddy Dutch, inspired this one. We simply asked him to request a cook. We had no idea how amazing it would be! It was so amazing that we had no choice but to share it with you. You've gotta make this one. Once you do, the Quad D will quickly become everyone's favorite.

1 tablespoon (14 g) butter

1 cup (115 g) sliced yellow onion

2 cups (140 g) mushrooms, sliced

1 tablespoon (15 ml) vegetable oil

1 pound (455 g) 80/20 ground beef, divided into four 4-ounce (115 g) loosely packed meatballs

2 teaspoons salt (to taste)

2 teaspoons pepper (to taste)

4 teaspoons (16 g) seasoned salt (We use Uncle Steve's Lucky Shake All Purpose or Lawry's Seasoned Salt.)

4 slices American cheese

2 hamburger buns

Mayonnaise, for topping

OPTIONAL:
additional 1 tablespoon (14 g) mayonnaise, for toasting the buns

1 Turn one side of the griddle on to medium/high to high heat (above 400°F [200°C]).

2 Turn the other side on to medium heat (350°F [180°C]).

3 Once the side of the griddle turned to medium heat is to temperature, lay the butter down, followed by the onions and mushrooms. Continue to cook until the onions are translucent and the mushrooms are soft.

4 Set the mushrooms and onions aside.

5 Once the side of the griddle turned to medium/high to high heat is to temperature, lay the oil on the griddle.

6 Place the 4 meatballs in the oil, ensuring space between the meatballs to give them room to be smashed.

7 Sprinkle salt and pepper liberally on the meatballs, followed by the seasoned salt.

If toasting the buns: While the griddle is coming up to temperature, spread the mayonnaise on the inside of the top and bottom buns and lay them on the griddle facedown. Pull the buns when they are a light golden brown and set aside.

8 After about 30 seconds, smash each meatball all the way down flat with a burger smasher or the back side of the spatula, using the back side of another spatula to help apply pressure. Hold the smash down for 10–15 seconds.

9 Once each burger is smashed and you see the juices begin to rise to the surface (almost immediately), use the spatula and quickly flip them and place a slice of American cheese on each burger.

10 Pull each burger from the heat. The cheese will continue to melt while building the burgers.

11 Place the burgers, stacking one on top of the other, on the bottom buns. Build in the following order: bottom bun, spread of mayonnaise, smash burger patties, mushrooms and onions. Spread mayonnaise on the top bun and place on top of the burger. Serve and enjoy!

Bacon Guacamole Smash Burger

SERVINGS: 1 burger | **PREP TIME:** 10 minutes | **COOK TIME:** 4 minutes (20 minutes if including bacon as part of the cook)

There's something about adding fresh guacamole and bacon to anything that makes it extra special. Here is your new most requested smash burger. Serve it with a side of Smashed Guacamole and some chips, and you have the perfect meal!

2 slices bacon

1 tablespoon (15 ml) vegetable oil

6–7 ounces (170 to 200 g) 80/20 ground beef, divided into two 3- to 3½-ounce (85 to 100 g) loosely packed meatballs

2 teaspoons salt (to taste)

2 teaspoons pepper (to taste)

2 slices provolone cheese

1 potato hamburger bun

Mayonnaise, for topping

1 tomato, sliced

½ red onion, thinly sliced

2 tablespoons (28 g) Smashed Guacamole, or your favorite guacamole (See recipe page 70.)

OPTIONAL:
additional 1 tablespoon (14 g) mayonnaise, for toasting the buns

Cook the bacon:

1 Turn the griddle on to medium heat (350°F [180°C]).

2 While the griddle is warming, place the strips of bacon on the griddle. (We have found that placing the bacon on the griddle before it is hot helps keep the bacon from curling too much.)

3 Cook the first side until browned and flip.

4 Continue to cook until the bacon is done to the desired crispiness. Pull and place on a paper towel–lined plate to drain off excess grease.

Cook the burgers:

1 Turn the griddle on to medium/high to high heat (above 400°F [200°C]).

2 Once the griddle is to temperature, lay the oil on the griddle.

3 Place the 2 meatballs in the oil, ensuring space between the meatballs to give them room to be smashed.

4 Sprinkle salt and pepper liberally on the meatballs. **CONTINUED →**

If toasting the buns: While the griddle is coming up to temperature, spread the mayonnaise on the inside of the top and bottom buns and lay them on the griddle facedown. Pull the buns when they are a light golden brown and set aside.

5 After about 30 seconds, smash each meatball all the way down flat with a burger smasher or the back side of the spatula, using the back side of another spatula to help apply pressure. Hold the smash down for 10–15 seconds.

6 Once each burger is smashed and you see the juices begin to rise to the surface (almost immediately), use the spatula and quickly flip them and place a slice of provolone cheese on each burger.

7 Pull each burger from the heat. The cheese will continue to melt while building the burger.

8 Place the burgers, stacking one on top of the other, on the bottom bun. Build in the following order: bottom bun, swirl of mayonnaise, smash burger patties, bacon, tomato, onion, Smashed Guacamole, top bun. Serve and enjoy!

Smashed Guacamole

½ red onion, diced
2 Roma tomatoes, diced
3 tablespoons (3 g) chopped cilantro
2 garlic cloves, minced
3 avocados (We have also used 5 petite avocados for this recipe.)
½ teaspoon sea salt
2 tablespoons (28 ml) lime juice
Optional: a bag of your favorite tortilla chips!

1 In a medium/large bowl, combine the diced onion, Roma tomatoes, cilantro, and garlic.

2 Cut open the avocados and remove the pits. Remove the avocado halves from peel and place in the bowl with other ingredients.

3 Add salt and lime juice.

4 Using a fork, mix all the ingredients together, mashing the avocado during the process. The key is to mash most of the avocado, while preserving some "chunks" for texture and taste. Add more salt/lime juice to taste.

Ground Ribeye Smash Burger

SERVINGS: 1 burger | **PREP TIME:** 15–20 minutes | **COOK TIME:** 4 minutes

We admit that it's tough to improve on a smash burger, but with ribeye, we have to make an exception. This will be the best smash burger you ever cook. . . or at least the most luxurious.

1 tablespoon (15 ml) vegetable oil

6–7 ounces (170 to 200 g) ground ribeye steak, divided into two 3- to 3½-ounce (85 to 100 g) loosely packed meatballs

2 teaspoons salt (to taste)

2 teaspoons pepper (to taste)

2 slices American cheese

1 potato hamburger bun

Ketchup, for topping

Mustard, for topping

Mayonnaise, for topping

4 dill pickle chips

Shredded lettuce, for topping

1 tomato, sliced

½ red onion, thinly sliced

OPTIONAL:
additional 1 tablespoon (14 g) mayonnaise, for toasting the buns

1 Turn the griddle on to medium/high to high heat (above 400°F [200°C]).

2 Once the griddle is to temperature, lay the oil on the griddle.

3 Place the 2 meatballs in the oil, ensuring space between the meatballs to give them room to be smashed.

4 Sprinkle salt and pepper liberally on the meatballs.

5 After about 30 seconds, smash each meatball all the way down flat with a burger smasher or the back side of the spatula, using the back side of another spatula to help apply pressure. Hold the smash down for 10–15 seconds.

6 Once each burger is smashed and you see the juices begin to rise to the surface (almost immediately), use the spatula and quickly flip them and place a slice of American cheese on each burger.

7 Pull each burger from the heat. The cheese will continue to melt while building the burger.

8 Place the burgers, stacking one on top of the other, on the bottom bun. Build in the following order (optional): bottom bun, swirl of ketchup, swirl of mustard, swirl of mayonnaise, pickle chips, lettuce, tomato, onion, smash burger patties, top bun. Serve and enjoy!

Peanut Butter Smash Burger

SERVINGS: 1 burger | **PREP TIME:** 10 minutes | **COOK TIME:** 4 minutes (if including bacon as part of the cook)

It's so weird, yet so good! We cannot explain why the flavors work, but they do. We were skeptical to try this one for ourselves, but it has only proven to inspire us to discover what else we can come up with combining ground beef and peanut butter.

2 slices bacon

1 tablespoon (15 ml) vegetable oil

6–7 ounces (170 to 200 g) 80/20 ground beef, divided into two 3- to 3½-ounce (85 to 100 g) loosely packed meatballs

2 teaspoons salt (to taste)

2 teaspoons pepper (to taste)

2 slices American cheese

1 potato hamburger bun

1 tablespoon (16 g) creamy peanut butter

4 dill pickle chips

OPTIONAL:
1 tablespoon (14 g) mayonnaise, for toasting the buns

Cook the bacon:

1 Turn the griddle on to medium heat (350°F [180°C]).

2 While the griddle is warming, place the strips of bacon on the griddle. (We have found that placing the bacon on the griddle before it is hot helps keep the bacon from curling too much.)

3 Cook the first side until browned and flip.

4 Continue to cook until the bacon is done to the desired crispiness. Pull and place on a paper towel–lined plate to drain off excess grease.

Cook the burger:

1 Turn the griddle on to medium/high to high heat (above 400°F [200°C]).

2 Once the griddle is to temperature, lay the oil on the griddle.

3 Place the 2 meatballs in the oil, ensuring space between the meatballs to give them room to be smashed.

4 Sprinkle salt and pepper liberally on the meatballs.

5 After about 30 seconds, smash each meatball all the way down flat with a burger smasher or the back side of the spatula, using the back side of another spatula to help apply pressure. Hold the smash down for 10–15 seconds.

6 Once each burger is smashed and you see the juices begin to rise to the surface (almost immediately), use the spatula and quickly flip them and place a slice of American cheese on each burger.

7 Pull each burger from the heat. The cheese will continue to melt while building the burger.

8 Place the burgers, stacking one on top of the other, and place on the bottom bun. Build in the following order: bottom bun, peanut butter, smash burger patties, bacon, pickle chips, top bun. Serve and enjoy!

~~~~~~~~~~~~~~~~~~~~~~~~~~~~~~~~~~~~~~

If toasting the buns: While the griddle is coming up to temperature, spread the mayonnaise on the inside of the top and bottom buns and lay them on the griddle facedown. Pull the buns when they are a light golden brown and set aside.

Mac 'n' Cheese Smash Burger

SERVINGS: 1 burger | **PREP TIME:** 10 minutes | **COOK TIME:** 4 minutes

Don't you love macaroni and cheese? We do too! Don't you also love smash burgers? No way, same here! Why not put them together? We did, and we gotta say, there's almost nothing like it. The cheesy goodness makes this mac 'n' cheeseburger one of the most substantial of all the smash burgers.

1 tablespoon (15 ml) vegetable oil

6–7 ounces (170 to 200 g) 80/20 ground beef, divided into two 3- to 3½-ounce (85 to 100 g) loosely packed meatballs

2 teaspoons salt (to taste)

2 teaspoons pepper (to taste)

2 slices American cheese

1 potato hamburger bun

1 recipe Mac and Cheese (See recipe on page 74.)

OPTIONAL:
additional 1 tablespoon (14 g) mayonnaise, for toasting the buns

1 Turn the griddle on to medium/high to high heat (above 400°F [200°C]).

2 Once the griddle is to temperature, lay the oil on the griddle.

3 Place the 2 meatballs in the oil, ensuring space between the meatballs to give them room to be smashed.

4 Sprinkle salt and pepper liberally on the meatballs.

5 After about 30 seconds, smash each meatball all the way down flat with a burger smasher or the back side of the spatula, using the back side of another spatula to help apply pressure. Hold the smash down for 10–15 seconds.

6 Once each burger is smashed and you see the juices begin to rise to the surface (almost immediately), use the spatula and quickly flip them and place a slice of American cheese on each burger.

7 Pull each burger from the heat. The cheese will continue to melt while building the burger.

8 Place the burgers, stacking one on top of the other, and place on the bottom bun. Build in the following order: bottom bun, a scoop of mac and cheese, smash burger patties, another scoop of mac and cheese, top bun. Serve and enjoy!

Mac and Cheese

8 cups (1.9 L) water
16 ounces (455 g) elbow macaroni
2 tablespoons (28 g) unsalted butter
2 tablespoons (16 g) all-purpose flour
2 cups (475 ml) whole milk
2 cups (226 g) shredded American cheese, or
    more if desired
½ cup (58 g) shredded cheddar cheese, or cheese
    of your choice
1¼ teaspoons salt, divided
1 teaspoon pepper

1 In a medium/large saucepan, bring 8 cups
   (1.9 L) of water and ¼ teaspoon of salt
   to a boil.

2 Once at a boil, add the elbow macaroni and
   continue boiling until the noodles are softened
   (about 8 minutes).

3 Drain the macaroni and set aside.

4 In a large saucepan over medium heat, melt
   the butter.

5 Once melted, stir in the flour and mix until it
   forms a roux and turns a light brown (about 30
   seconds to a minute). Add 1 cup (235 ml) of
   milk slowly while stirring. Once the milk begins
   to thicken, add an additional cup (235 ml) of
   milk and begin adding the shredded American
   cheese. Add the American cheese in slowly,
   small amounts at a time, and stir. Once the
   cheese is melted, add more.

6 Once all the American cheese is melted, add
   the shredded cheddar cheese, 1 teaspoon of
   salt, and pepper, continuing to stir. Once the
   cheddar cheese is melted and you have desired
   thickness (when cheese easily sticks to a
   spoon), add the elbow macaroni to the cheese
   sauce and mix thoroughly.

Cheddar on Rye Smash Burger

SERVINGS: 1 burger | **PREP TIME:** 10 minutes | **COOK TIME:** 4 minutes

There's something about the combination of cheddar cheese on rye bread that just works so well together. Add 80/20 ground beef smashed into the perfect burger, and you've got one of the heartiest smash burgers there is!

1 tablespoon (14 g) unsalted butter

2 slices rye bread

1 tablespoon (15 ml) vegetable oil

6–7 ounces (170 to 200 g) 80/20 ground beef, divided into two 3- to 3½-ounce (85 to 100 g) loosely packed meatballs

2 teaspoons salt (to taste)

2 teaspoons pepper (to taste)

2 slices cheddar cheese

Mustard, for topping

Mayonnaise, for topping

4 dill pickle chips

Shredded lettuce, for topping

½ red onion, thinly sliced

1 tomato, sliced

1 Turn the griddle on to medium/high to high heat (above 400°F [200°C]).

2 While the griddle is coming up to temperature, spread the butter on 1 side of each slice of bread and lay butter-side down on the griddle. Once the bread is toasted to a light golden brown, pull and set aside.

3 Once the griddle is to temperature, lay the oil on the griddle.

4 Place the 2 meatballs in the oil, ensuring space between the meatballs to give them room to be smashed.

5 Sprinkle salt and pepper liberally on the meatballs.

6 After about 30 seconds, smash each meatball all the way down flat with a burger smasher or the back side of the spatula, using the back side of another spatula to help apply pressure. Hold the smash down for 10–15 seconds.

7 Once each burger is smashed and you see the juices begin to rise to the surface (almost immediately), use the spatula and quickly flip them and place a slice of cheddar cheese on each burger.

8 Pull each burger from the heat. The cheese will continue to melt while building the burger.

9 Place the burgers, stacking one on top of the other, on the bottom slice of bread. Build in the following order (optional): bottom slice of bread, swirl of mustard, swirl of mayonnaise, smash burger patties, pickle chips, lettuce, onion, tomato, top slice of bread. Serve and enjoy!

Grilled Cheese Smash Burger

SERVINGS: 1 burger | **PREP TIME:** 10 minutes | **COOK TIME:** 8–10 minutes

The perfect grilled cheese meets the perfect smash burger, and it's all buttery toasted bread, luscious cheddar cheese, and savory ground beef. Add your favorite toppings, and you may choose to never make a burger another way again.

2 tablespoons (28 g) butter

4 thick slices white bread

½ cup (115 g) shredded cheddar cheese

1 tablespoon (15 ml) vegetable oil

5 ounces (140 g) 80/20 ground beef, divided into two 2½-ounce (70 g) loosely packed meatballs

2 teaspoons salt (to taste)

2 teaspoons pepper (to taste)

2 slices American cheese

1 tablespoon (14 g) mayonnaise

5 dill pickle chips

1 tablespoon (15 g) ketchup

1 Turn the griddle on to medium/high to high heat (above 400°F [200°C]).

2 Once the griddle is around 400°F [200°C], lay down two pats of butter and move them around until fully melted on the surface. Place 2 slices of bread on the melted butter, add ¼ cup (30 g) of shredded cheddar cheese on top of each slice, and place the other 2 slices of bread on top of the cheese. After a couple of minutes, check to make sure that the bottom is starting to brown and the cheese is melting.

3 Once the bottom slices of bread are golden brown, lay down 2 more pats of butter and flip the sandwiches.

4 Once the second slices of bread are golden brown and the cheese is melted, pull the sandwiches and set aside. These grilled cheese sandwiches will be the bun for the smash burger!

5 Lay the oil on the griddle. Place the 2 meatballs in the oil, ensuring space between the meatballs to give them room to be smashed.

6 Sprinkle salt and pepper liberally on the meatballs.

7 After about 30 seconds, smash each meatball all the way down flat with a burger smasher or the back side of the spatula, using the back side of another spatula to help apply pressure. Hold the smash down for 10–15 seconds.

8 Once each burger is smashed and you see the juices begin to rise to the surface (almost immediately), use the spatula and quickly flip them and place a slice of American cheese on each burger.

9 Pull each burger from the heat, stacking one on top of the other, and place on a plate. The cheese will continue to melt while building the burger.

10 Spread mayonnaise on one of the grilled cheese sandwiches and place the smash burger patties on top. Place the pickle chips on top of the burger, spread ketchup on the other grilled cheese sandwich, and place on top of the burger. Serve and enjoy!

Do Your Prep!

Remember, the griddle cooks hot and fast, having everything with you BEFORE you start cooking is key! You don't want to be running back into the house having forgotten something while the food's cooking.

Poutine Smash Burger with Homemade Griddle Fries

SERVINGS: 2 burgers | **PREP TIME:** 10 minutes | **COOK TIME:** 15–20 minutes

Thank you, Canada! Yes, we mean to thank the entire country for giving us such amazing savory flavors as those found in poutine! We put all that goodness on a smash burger! No matter how you pronounce "poutine," we say it's spectacularly delicious!

GRIDDLE FRIES

1 large Russet potato, cut into ¼-inch x ¼-inch (3 mm x 3 mm) strips

2–4 tablespoons (28 to 60 ml) peanut oil

1 tablespoon (18 g) salt

POUTINE SMASH BURGER

1 package (1 ounce, or 28 g) brown gravy mix (We use McCormick's Brown Gravy mix.)

1 cup (235 ml) water

1 tablespoon (15 ml) vegetable oil

12 ounces (340 g) 80/20 ground beef, divided into four 3-ounce (85 g) loosely packed meatballs

2 teaspoons salt (to taste)

2 teaspoons pepper (to taste)

2 potato hamburger buns

1 package (16 ounces, or 455 g) cheese curds (We use Ellsworth Cheese Curds.)

Cook the griddle fries:

1 Soak the fries in cold water for 5–10 minutes. After soaking, pull from the water, lay flat onto a dry paper towel, and cover with another dry paper towel and pat dry.

2 Turn one side of the griddle on to medium/low heat (300°F to 325°F [150°C to 170°C]).

3 Turn the other side of the griddle on to medium/high heat (375 to 400°F [190 to 200°C]).

4 Pour 1–2 tablespoons (15 to 28 ml) of peanut oil onto the medium/low heat side of the griddle, letting it settle to create a "griddle fry."

5 Place half of the fries flat onto the oil and start to cook. Once they start to turn light brown, remove from the griddle and let rest for about 2 minutes.

6 Repeat with the second half of the fries, placing them on the oil.

7 Pour 1–2 tablespoons (15 to 28 ml) of peanut oil onto the medium/high heat side of the griddle and place the first batch of fries onto the oil. CONTINUED →

8 Once they are GBD (golden, brown, and delicious), pull off the griddle and salt.

9 Repeat with the rest of the fries.

Prepare the gravy:

1 In a small pot, pour in the gravy packet and slowly pour 1 cup (235 ml) water, stirring at the same time.

2 Once the gravy starts to boil, stir well, and pull from the griddle.

Cook the burgers:

1 Turn the griddle on to medium/high to high heat (above 400°F [200°C]).

2 Once the griddle is to temperature, lay the oil on the griddle.

3 Place the 4 meatballs on the griddle, ensuring space between the meatballs to give them room to be smashed.

4 Sprinkle salt and pepper liberally on the meatballs.

5 After about 30 seconds, smash each meatball all the way down flat with a burger smasher or the back side of the spatula, using the back side of another spatula to help apply pressure. Hold the smash down for 10–15 seconds.

6 Once each burger is smashed and you see the juices begin to rise to the surface (almost immediately), use the spatula and quickly flip them. Cook for an additional minute.

7 Pull each burger from the heat.

8 Place the burgers, stacking one on top of the other, on the bottom buns. Place a handful of fries on each burger, followed by a small handful of cheese curds on top of the fries, and pour approximately 2 tablespoons (30 g) of gravy onto each stack. Place the top bun on the burgers. Serve and enjoy!

Copycat Big Mac— Smash Burger Style!

SERVINGS: 1 burger | **PREP TIME:** 10 minutes | **COOK TIME:** 4 minutes

We would never be so bold as to claim that our version is better than the original. Wait a minute. Yes, we would. We think our Copycat Big Mac Smash Burger is better than the original Big Mac. Sorry, McDonald's.

1 sesame seed hamburger bun, plus an additional bottom bun cut to make an even "inner" bun

1 tablespoon (15 ml) vegetable oil

6–7 ounces (170 to 200 g) 80/20 ground beef, divided into two 3- to 3½-ounce (85 to 100 g) loosely packed meatballs

2 teaspoons salt (to taste)

2 teaspoons pepper (to taste)

2 tablespoons (30 g) Copycat Big Mac Sauce (See recipe on page 85.)

2 tablespoons (20 g) diced white onion

½ cup (22 g) shredded iceberg lettuce

1 slice American cheese

4 dill pickle chips

1   Turn the griddle on to medium/high to high heat (above 400°F [200°C]).

2   While the griddle is coming up to temperature, lay the top and bottom buns on the griddle facedown. Once the buns are toasted to a light golden brown, pull and set aside.

3   Once the griddle is to temperature, lay the oil on the griddle.

4   Place the 2 meatballs in the oil, ensuring space between the meatballs to give them room to be smashed.

5   Sprinkle salt and pepper liberally on the meatballs.

6   After about 30 seconds, smash each meatball all the way down flat with a burger smasher or the back side of the spatula, using the back side of another spatula to help apply pressure. Hold the smash down for 10–15 seconds.

7   Once each burger is smashed and you see the juices begin to rise to the surface (almost immediately), use the spatula and quickly flip them.

8   Pull each burger from the heat.

9   Build the Copycat Big Mac Smash Burger in the following order: bottom bun, spread of Copycat Big Mac Sauce, a small amount of onions and lettuce, followed by the American cheese and one smash burger patty. On the burger, place the "inner" bun, followed by another spread of Copycat Big Mac Sauce, lettuce, and the pickles. **CONTINUED ➜**

10 Place the second smash burger patty, followed by the remaining onions, and place the top bun on top of the burger. Serve and enjoy!

Copycat Big Mac Sauce

¼ cup (60 g) mayonnaise
2 tablespoons (30 g) ketchup
2 tablespoons (30 g) dill pickle relish
  with juice

Mix all the ingredients together until evenly mixed and chill in the refrigerator for at least 30 minutes.

CHAPTER 2

SUPER SMASHED CHICKEN BURGERS

THE RECIPES

* Yes, this is a pork smash in the chicken chapter. But we couldn't separate these last two—they are classics. Don't tell the publisher. It'll be our secret . . .

Chicken Cordon Bleu Smash Burger

SERVINGS: 2 burgers | **PREP TIME:** 10 minutes | **COOK TIME:** 4 minutes

The perfect balance of chicken, ham, Swiss cheese, and honey mustard will guarantee that this becomes your new favorite way to Cordon Bleu.

1 tablespoon (14 g) mayonnaise

2 potato hamburger buns

1 tablespoon (15 ml) vegetable oil

12 ounces (340 g) ground chicken, divided into four 3-ounce (85 g) loosely packed meatballs

4 teaspoons (14 g) Usual Suspects Seasoning (See recipe on page 111.)

4 slices Swiss cheese

4 slices deli sliced honey ham

2 tablespoons (30 g) honey mustard

OPTIONAL:
additional mayonnaise, for topping

Note: If you want it a bit creamier, put a spread of mayonnaise on the inside top bun before topping.

1 Turn the griddle on to medium heat (350°F [180°C]).

2 While the griddle is coming up to temperature, spread mayonnaise on the inside of each of the buns and place on the griddle facedown. Once the buns are toasted to a light golden brown, pull and set aside.

3 Once the griddle is to temperature, lay the oil on the griddle.

4 Place the 4 chicken meatballs in the oil, ensuring space between the meatballs to give them room to be smashed. Sprinkle the Usual Suspects Seasoning liberally on the meatballs.

5 After about 30 seconds, smash each meatball all the way down flat with a burger smasher or the back side of the spatula, using the back side of another spatula to help apply pressure. Hold the smash down for 10–15 seconds.

6 Once each burger is smashed, use the spatula and quickly flip them and place a slice of Swiss cheese on each burger.

7 Pull each burger from the heat. The cheese will continue to melt while building the burgers.

8 Place the burgers, stacking one on top of the other, and place on the bottom buns.

9 Place the ham on the griddle for about 45 seconds to get hot.

10 Pull the ham and place on the burgers. Put a swirl of honey mustard on top of the ham and place the top bun. Serve and enjoy!

Nashville Hot Chicken Smash Burger

SERVINGS: 2 burgers | **PREP TIME:** 10 minutes | **COOK TIME:** 4–6 minutes

The first time we tried making Nashville Hot, we were blown away. We cannot believe how incredibly packed with flavor this zesty and refreshing smash burger is!

1 tablespoon (14 g) mayonnaise, plus additional for topping

2 potato hamburger buns

1 tablespoon (15 ml) vegetable oil

12 ounces (340 g) ground chicken, divided into four 3-ounce (85 g) loosely packed meatballs

4 teaspoons (14 g) Usual Suspects Seasoning (See recipe on page 111.)

1 recipe Nashville Hot Sauce (See recipe on page 93.)

8 dill pickle chips

1 Turn the griddle on to medium heat (350°F [180°C]).

2 While the griddle is coming up to temperature, spread mayonnaise on the inside of each of the buns and place on the griddle facedown. Once the buns are toasted to a light golden brown, pull and set aside.

3 Once the griddle is to temperature, lay the oil on the griddle.

4 Place the 4 chicken meatballs in the oil, ensuring space between the meatballs to give them room to be smashed.

5 Sprinkle the Usual Suspects Seasoning liberally on the meatballs.

6 After about 30 seconds, smash each meatball all the way down flat with a burger smasher or the back side of the spatula, using the back side of another spatula to help apply pressure. Hold the smash down for 10–15 seconds.

7 Once each burger is smashed, use the spatula and quickly flip them.

8 Pull each burger from the heat and submerge in the Nashville Hot Sauce.

9 After a dunk in the Nashville Hot Sauce, place the burgers, stacking one on top of the other, on the bottom buns. Top with 4 dill pickle chips. Add a spread of mayonnaise on the inside of the top buns and place on top of the burgers. Serve and enjoy!

Nashville Hot Sauce

2 tablespoons (10 g) cayenne pepper
1½ tablespoons (23 g) brown sugar
   (We added a bit more for added sweetness.)
½ teaspoon chili powder
½ teaspoon garlic powder
½ cup (120 ml) vegetable oil

Mix all the ingredients together and set aside in
a shallow bowl.

Chicken Bacon Ranch Pressed Smash Burger

SERVINGS: 2 burgers | **PREP TIME:** 10 minutes | **COOK TIME:** 4 minutes (20 minutes if including bacon as part of the cook)

Do you ever find yourself craving something savory but also bright and fresh? Well, we've got you covered with the perfect chicken smash burger that is exceptionally satisfying to the last bite!

1 tablespoon (15 ml) vegetable oil

12 ounces (340 g) ground chicken, divided into four 3-ounce (85 g) loosely packed meatballs

1–1½ teaspoons salt, divided (to taste)

1–1½ teaspoons pepper, divided (to taste)

4 slices Swiss cheese

2 ciabatta rolls, split in half

1–2 Roma tomatoes, sliced

4 slices cooked bacon

¼ cup (60 g) ranch dressing

Note: A heavy cast iron or other large grill/griddle press is best suited for use with this sandwich.

1 Turn the griddle on to medium/high to high heat (above 400°F [200°C]).

2 Once the griddle is to temperature, lay the oil on the griddle.

3 Place the 4 meatballs in the oil, ensuring space between the meatballs to give them room to be smashed. Sprinkle salt and pepper liberally on the meatballs.

4 After about 30 seconds, smash each meatball all the way down flat with a burger smasher or the back side of the spatula, using the back side of another spatula to help apply pressure. Hold the smash down for 10–15 seconds.

5 Once each burger is smashed, use the spatula and quickly flip them and place a slice of Swiss cheese on each burger.

6 Pull each burger from the heat. The cheese will continue to melt while building the burgers.

7 Place the burgers, stacking one on top of the other, on the bottom rolls. Build in the following order: bottom roll, smash chicken burgers, tomatoes, sprinkled with ½ teaspoon each of salt and pepper, bacon, a drizzle of ranch dressing, top roll. Place a grill/griddle press on top of the sandwich for about 1 minute. Once the bottom roll is lightly browned, carefully flip the burger and press, being careful not to split the roll. Once the top roll is lightly browned, carefully flip back over and pull from the heat. Serve and enjoy!

Pressed Chicken Cheesesteak

SERVINGS: 4 sandwiches | **PREP TIME:** 15 minutes | **COOK TIME:** 10 minutes

We've said it before, and we'll say it again—chicken cheesesteak may be one of our all-time favorite cheesesteaks! This pressed version adds an intensity of flavor that can't be explained. Try it and you'll see what we mean.

2 tablespoons (28 ml) vegetable oil, divided

3 tablespoons (42 g) unsalted butter

1 large yellow onion, diced

2 teaspoons salt, divided

2 teaspoons pepper, divided

1 pound (455 g) chicken breast, cut into 1-inch (2.5 cm) cubes

12 slices provolone cheese

4 hoagie rolls, sliced

Note: A heavy cast iron or other large grill/griddle press is best suited for use with this sandwich.

1 Turn the griddle on to medium/low heat (300 to 325°F [150°C to 170°C]).

2 Lay 1 tablespoon (15 ml) of oil on the griddle, followed by the butter. As soon as the butter is melted, place the onions in the butter and add 1 teaspoon each of salt and pepper. Continue to cook, moving slowly until the onions begin to turn translucent (about 5–6 minutes). Move the onions to a cooler side of the griddle or pull and set aside.

3 Once the griddle is to temperature, lay the remaining vegetable oil on the griddle.

4 Place the cubed chicken in the oil. Add 1 teaspoon of salt and 1 teaspoon of pepper. Once the chicken begins to cook through, stir and "chop" the chicken with a scraper to break it up into small chunks and pieces. Continue to stir until the chicken is thoroughly cooked.

5 Mix the chicken in with the onions and divide the meat and onions into 4 even lines (equivalent to the length of the hoagie). Lay 3 slices of pro-volone cheese on each line. With the spatula, scoop up a line of chicken, onions, and cheese and place in hoagie roll. Repeat for each chicken cheesesteak.

6 Place the filled hoagie rolls on the griddle and place a large grill/griddle press on top of the sandwiches. You do not need to press down, but just allow the press to slightly flatten the sandwiches. Once the bottom of the rolls are golden brown and toasted, flip and repeat the same cooking process on the second side.

7 Pull the sandwiches from the heat and slice in half. Serve and enjoy!

Buffalo Chicken Cheesesteak

SERVINGS: 4 sandwiches | **PREP TIME:** 15 minutes | **COOK TIME:** 10 minutes

How can you make a Chicken Cheesesteak even better? By adding Buffalo sauce, of course! We added plenty of spicy Buffalo sauce to heat things up and then topped it with creamy ranch dressing to cool things down. It's like those chicken wings you love so much, only nestled in a toasty hoagie roll and covered with cheese . . . so, what are you waiting for?

1 tablespoon (15 ml) vegetable oil

1 pound (455 g) chicken breast, cut into 1-inch (2.5 cm) cubes

4 teaspoons (14 g) Usual Suspects Seasoning (See recipe on page 111.)

½ cup (120 ml) Buffalo sauce, or more (We use Frank's RedHot Buffalo Wing Sauce.)

12 slices provolone cheese

4 hoagie rolls, sliced

¼ cup (60 g) ranch dressing, or blue cheese dressing

1 Turn the griddle on to medium/low heat (300 to 325°F [150°C to 170°C]).

2 Once the griddle is to temperature, lay the oil on the griddle.

3 Place the cubed chicken in the oil. Sprinkle liberally with the Usual Suspects Seasoning. Once the chicken begins to cook through, stir and "chop" the chicken with a scraper to break it up into small chunks and pieces. Continue to stir until the chicken is thoroughly cooked.

4 Add the Buffalo sauce and mix in. Divide the meat into 4 even lines (equivalent to the length of the hoagie) and lay 3 slices of provolone cheese on each line.

5 Cover all 4 piles with a dome to ensure that the cheese melts.

6 Place the hoagie rolls on the griddle for about a minute to heat up the outside of each roll.

7 Remove the dome. Open each roll and lay cut-side down on each line of cheesesteak. Let sit for about 30 seconds and then with a spatula, scoop up the cheesesteak, holding firm to the hoagie, and turn the whole sandwich right-side up.

8 Pull the sandwiches from the heat, drizzle liberally with ranch dressing, and slice in half. Serve and enjoy!

Buffalo Chicken Smash Burger

SERVINGS: 2 burgers | **PREP TIME:** 15 minutes | **COOK TIME:** 4–6 minutes

We had you at Buffalo Chicken, right? This chicken smash burger version takes your beloved wings and transforms them into a creative option for a delicious dinner, or for a hearty lunch, or maybe even . . . for an eye-opening breakfast? Go ahead. We won't judge.

1 tablespoon (14 g) mayonnaise, plus an additional ½ tablespoon for topping

2 potato hamburger buns

1 tablespoon (15 ml) vegetable oil

12 ounces (340 g) ground chicken, divided into four 3-ounce (85 g) loosely packed meatballs

4 teaspoons (14 g) Usual Suspects Seasoning (See recipe on page 111.)

4 slices provolone cheese

8 dill pickle chips

2 tablespoons (28 ml) Buffalo sauce (We use Frank's RedHot Buffalo Wing Sauce.)

½ cup (115 g) shredded lettuce

1 tomato, sliced

½ red onion, thinly sliced

2 tablespoons (30 g) ranch dressing, or blue cheese dressing

1 Turn the griddle on to medium heat (350°F [180°C]).

2 While the griddle is coming up to temperature, spread mayonnaise on the inside of each of the buns and place on the griddle facedown. Once the buns are toasted to a light golden brown, pull and set aside.

3 Once the griddle is to temperature, lay the oil on the griddle.

4 Place the 4 chicken meatballs in the oil, ensuring space between the meatballs to give them room to be smashed. Sprinkle the Usual Suspects Seasoning liberally on the meatballs.

5 After about 30 seconds, smash each meatball all the way down flat with a burger smasher or the back side of the spatula, using the back side of another spatula to help apply pressure. Hold the smash down for 10–15 seconds.

6 Once each burger is smashed, use the spatula and quickly flip them and place a slice of provolone cheese on each burger.

7 Pull each burger from the heat. The cheese will continue to melt while building the burgers.

8 Place the burgers, stacking one on top of the other, on the bottom buns. Build in the following order: bottom bun, swirl of mayonnaise, 4 pickle chips, smash chicken burgers, Buffalo sauce, lettuce, tomato, onion, ranch dressing, top bun. Serve and enjoy!

Classic Chicken Smash Burger

SERVINGS: 2 burgers | **PREP TIME:** 10 minutes | **COOK TIME:** 4 minutes

There are times when we absolutely have a hankering for a smashed chicken burger. It's a lighter overall profile but still incredibly gratifying. We believe everyone needs the Classic Chicken Smash Burger in their smash arsenal!

1 tablespoon (14 g) mayonnaise, plus additional for topping

2 potato hamburger buns

1 tablespoon (15 ml) vegetable oil

12 ounces (340 g) ground chicken, divided into four 3-ounce (85 g) loosely packed meatballs

4 teaspoons (14 g) Usual Suspects Seasoning (See recipe on page 111.)

4 slices provolone cheese

Mustard, for topping

8 dill pickle chips

Shredded lettuce, for topping

1 tomato, sliced

½ red onion, thinly sliced

1. Turn the griddle on to medium heat (350°F [180°C]).

2. While the griddle is coming up to temperature, spread mayonnaise on the inside of each of the buns and place on the griddle facedown. Once the buns are toasted to a light golden brown, pull and set aside.

3. Once the griddle is to temperature, lay the oil on the griddle.

4. Place the 4 chicken meatballs in the oil, ensuring space between the meatballs to give them room to be smashed.

5. Sprinkle the Usual Suspects Seasoning liberally on the meatballs.

6. After about 30 seconds, smash each meatball all the way down flat with a burger smasher or the back side of the spatula, using the back side of another spatula to help apply pressure. Hold the smash down for 10–15 seconds.

7. Once each burger is smashed, use the spatula and quickly flip them and place a slice of provolone cheese on each burger.

8. Pull each burger from the heat. The cheese will continue to melt while building the burgers.

9. Place the burgers, stacking one on top of the other, on the bottom buns. Build in the following order (optional): bottom bun, swirl of mustard, swirl of mayonnaise, 4 pickle chips, smash chicken burgers, lettuce, tomato, onion, top bun. Serve and enjoy!

Classic Ground Pork Smash Burger

SERVINGS: 2 burgers | **PREP TIME:** 10 minutes | **COOK TIME:** 4 minutes

The slight difference in texture and flavor makes the Classic Ground Pork Smash Burger a standout. Add your favorite BBQ sauce, and you take this one to the next level!

12 ounces (340 g) ground pork mixture, divided into four 3-ounce (85 g) loosely packed meatballs

1 egg

¼ cup (30 g) bread crumbs

1 tablespoon (14 g) mayonnaise

2 potato hamburger buns

1 tablespoon (15 ml) vegetable oil

4 teaspoons (14 g) Usual Suspects Seasoning (See recipe on page 111.)

4 slices gouda cheese

Garlic aioli, or additional mayonnaise, for topping

8 dill pickle chips

Shredded lettuce, for topping

1 tomato, sliced

½ red onion, thinly sliced

Note: "No, it's not chicken—but we had to put this amazing pork burger *somewhere* in the book!"

1 Turn the griddle on to medium heat (350°F [180°C]).

2 Prepare the ground pork by mixing 12 ounces (340 g) of ground pork, 1 egg, and ¼ cup of (30 g) bread crumbs. Mix together until the egg and bread crumbs are evenly mixed throughout the pork and divide into 4 loosely packed meatballs.

3 While the griddle is coming up to temperature, spread mayonnaise on the inside of each of the buns and place on the griddle facedown. Once the buns are toasted to a light golden brown, pull and set aside.

4 Once the griddle is to temperature, lay the oil on the griddle. Place the 4 pork meatballs in the oil, ensuring space between the meatballs to give them room to be smashed. Sprinkle the Usual Suspects Seasoning liberally on the meatballs. After about 30 seconds, smash each meatball all the way down flat with a burger smasher or the back side of the spatula, using the back side of another spatula to help apply pressure. Hold the smash down for 10–15 seconds.

5 Once each burger is smashed, use the spatula and quickly flip them and place a slice of gouda cheese on each burger. Pull each burger from the heat. The cheese will continue to melt while building the burgers.

6 Place the burgers, stacking one on top of the other, on the bottom buns. Build in the following order (optional): bottom bun, swirl of garlic aioli or mayonnaise, 4 pickle chips, smash pork burgers, lettuce, tomato, onion, top bun. Serve and enjoy!

CHAPTER 3

PRESSED PANINIS, SMASHED BURRITOS, AND WICKED WRAPS & SAMMIES

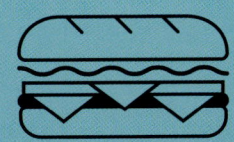

THE RECIPES

Pressed Chicken Street Quesadilla

SERVINGS: 4-5 quesadillas | **PREP TIME:** 10-15 minutes | **COOK TIME:** 8-10 minutes

The first time we made chicken street tacos, we were sold on the bold flavors. This pressed quesadilla gives that street taco a unique flavor profile that is perfect as an appetizer, a full meal, or anytime!

2 tablespoons (24 g) Tajin Seasoning, or a homemade Mexican Spice Blend (See recipe on page 107.)

1 tablespoon (10.5 g) Usual Suspects Seasoning (See recipe on page 111.)

2 pounds (900 g) boneless skinless chicken thighs

1 tablespoon (15 ml) vegetable oil

3 limes, quartered

2 tablespoons (28 g) unsalted butter

8-10 street taco flour tortillas

2 cups (225 g) shredded Mexican cheese blend

Creamy Jalapeño Ranch Dressing (See recipe on page 107.)

½ cup (8 g) chopped cilantro

Note: A heavy cast iron or other large grill/griddle press is best suited for use with this sandwich.

1 Combine the Tajin Seasoning and Usual Suspects Seasoning together and set aside

2 Before cooking, pound the chicken thigh meat out as flat as possible (⅛ to ¼ inch [3 to 6 mm] in thickness) without breaking or tearing the meat.

3 Turn the griddle on to medium/low heat (300 to 325°F [150°C to 170°C]).

4 Once the griddle is to temperature, lay the oil on the griddle.

5 Place the chicken thighs in the oil.

6 Cook for about 2-3 minutes or until the chicken is halfway cooked from the bottom (it will be a light brown color halfway up). At this point, season the top side liberally with about half of the Tajin/Usual Suspects mix and squeeze 1 of the limes onto the chicken. Flip the chicken thighs and use the remaining seasoning mix and another of the limes on the second side.

7 Continue cooking for an additional 2 minutes or until the internal temperature reaches at least 165°F (74°C). Pull the chicken and let it rest for 5 minutes.

8 Slice the chicken thigh meat into ¼-inch (6 mm) strips.

9 In a cleared area on the griddle, place half of the butter. Place half of the tortillas on the butter. On each tortilla, place a small handful of shredded Mexican cheese, 3-4 strips of chicken, more shredded cheese, and top with the remaining tortillas. Place a grill/griddle press on top of the quesadillas and cook until the bottom tortillas begin to brown.

Creamy Jalapeño Ranch Dressing

1 package (1 ounce, or 28 g) ranch dressing mix, prepared per package instructions (We use Hidden Valley Ranch Dressing, Dip, & Sauce Mix.)
½ medium jalapeño, deseeded and finely chopped
2 tablespoons (2 g) finely chopped cilantro
1–2 teaspoons dill pickle juice (to taste)
1–2 tablespoons (15 to 28 ml) lime juice

Mix all the ingredients well and chill in the refrigerator at least 30 minutes before serving.

Mexican Spice Blend

2 teaspoons salt
¼ teaspoon chili powder
Squeeze of fresh lime juice

Mix the salt and chili powder together with a squeeze of fresh lime.

10 Remove the press and spread the remaining butter on the top of each quesadilla and carefully flip. Place the press back on the quesadillas and cook for an additional 1–2 minutes or until the bottom tortillas are lightly browned and the cheese is melted.

11 Pull from the griddle, cut into 4 equal triangles, and serve with a side of Creamy Jalapeño Ranch Dressing and cilantro. Enjoy!

"Classic" Italian Panini

SERVINGS: 1 sandwich | **PREP TIME:** 3 minutes | **COOK TIME:** 5 minutes

The Panini originated in Italy, so we felt it necessary to include a classic Italian. Also, we wanted an excuse to share this mouth-watering sandwich! The toppings listed here are our preferences. Feel free to dress the sandwich to your liking.

1 tablespoon (14 g) unsalted butter

1 small ciabatta bread, split in half

2 slices provolone cheese

2 slices deli sliced Black Forest Ham

2 slices deli sliced genoa salami

2 slices deli sliced roasted turkey breast

Sliced tomato, for topping

Shredded lettuce, for topping

Red onion, thinly sliced, for topping

Banana peppers, sliced, for topping

1 tablespoon (15 ml) Italian dressing

Salt and pepper (to taste)

OPTIONAL:
dill pickle spear to serve on the side

1. Turn the griddle on to medium/low heat (300 to 325°F [150°C to 170°C]).

2. While the griddle is coming up to temperature, spread the butter on the inside slices of the ciabatta bread.

3. Lay the bread butter-side down on the griddle.

4. Once the bread is lightly browned, pull the top slice of bread and set aside. Turn the bottom slice over and begin building the sandwich in the following order: provolone cheese, ham, salami, turkey breast, tomato, lettuce, onion, banana peppers, Italian dressing, salt and pepper to taste, top slice of ciabatta bread.

5. Place a large grill/griddle press on top of the sandwich. You do not need to apply pressure if using a cast iron press. Let sit for 2–3 minutes or until the bottom slice of bread is golden brown.

6. Carefully flip the sandwich, lay the press again, and repeat the same cooking process on the second side (about 2 additional minutes).

7. Pull from the griddle, slice, and add a pickle spear on the side. Serve and enjoy!

Note: A heavy cast iron or other large grill/griddle press is best suited for use with this sandwich.

Chicken Caesar Salad Wrap

SERVINGS: 2 wraps | **PREP TIME:** 10 minutes | **COOKING TIME:** 15–20 minutes

Who'd have thought that putting a salad inside a tortilla would make it your new favorite salad? We did. The WALTWINS. We knew this would be your new fave. You're welcome.

½ head Romaine lettuce, chopped

1 cup (30 g) Italian seasoned croutons

Freshly grated Parmesan cheese

½ cup (120 g) Caesar dressing

5 boneless skinless chicken thighs, approximately 1 pound (455 g), flattened with tenderizer

2 tablespoons (21 g) Usual Suspects Seasoning (See recipe on page 111.)

1 tablespoon (15 ml) vegetable oil

2 spinach tortilla wraps

Note: A heavy cast iron or other large grill/griddle press is best suited for use with this sandwich.

1 Turn the griddle on to medium/low heat (300 to 325°F [150°C to 170°C]).

2 While the griddle is warming, place the lettuce, croutons, grated Parmesan cheese, and Caesar dressing in a large bowl and mix, ensuring everything is coated evenly. Set aside.

3 Season the chicken with the Usual Suspects Seasoning.

4 Once the griddle is to temperature, lay the oil on the griddle.

5 Place the chicken on the griddle and cook until the bottom begins to brown (about 4 minutes). Turn the chicken and cook the other side until the internal temperature of the chicken reaches at least 170°F (77°C).

6 Pull the chicken and let sit for 5 minutes (to cool a bit before combining with the salad mix).

7 Once it has cooled slightly, add the chicken to the salad mix and mix together, ensuring even distribution. If needed, add more Caesar Dressing.

8 Place approximately ½ cup (120 ml) of the salad and chicken mixture in the middle of each tortilla.

9 Wrap the tortillas: Fold in sides of each tortilla about 1 to 2 inches (2.5 to 5 cm) inward. With the sides still folded in, use your thumbs to pull the tortilla flap closest to you and lift it up and over the filling. While rolling the tortilla up and over the filling, keep the tortilla relatively tight and continue to roll until the wrap is secure.

10 Place the wraps on the griddle and place a grill/griddle press on top of the wraps. Let sit for about 1 minute or until the bottoms begin to turn golden brown. Flip the wraps and repeat the same cooking process on the second side.

11 Cut the wraps in the center diagonally. Serve and enjoy!

Usual Suspects Seasoning

1 tablespoon (18 g) salt
½ tablespoon pepper
½ tablespoon onion powder
1 tablespoon (9 g) garlic powder
½ tablespoon adobo seasoning
1 tablespoon (12 g) Accent Flavor Enhancer

Mix all the ingredients together in a shaker and set aside.

Pressed Beef Burrito

SERVINGS: 4 burritos | **PREP TIME:** 10 minutes | **COOK TIME:** 10–15 minutes

There's something about heat-pressing everything that takes it to the next level of flavor! The crispy perfection of a pressed tortilla makes any burrito better. Once you try it, this will become your new go-to burrito recipe!

2 tablespoons (28 ml) vegetable oil

1 pound (455 g) 80/20 ground beef

1 packet (1 ounce, or 28 g) taco seasoning

4 burrito-size tortillas

½ cup (104 g) queso dip

1 cup (120 g) shredded cheddar cheese, divided into ¼ cup (30 g) portions

4 tablespoons (60 g) sour cream

1 package (5.6 ounces, or 160 g) of Spanish or Mexican rice, prepared

Crispy tortilla strips

1 large tomato, sliced

Note: A heavy cast iron or other large grill/griddle press is best suited for use with this sandwich.

1 Turn the griddle on to medium/low heat (300 to 325°F [150°C to 170°C]).

2 Once the griddle is to temperature, lay the oil on the griddle, followed by the ground beef. Cook until browned (approximately 4–5 minutes).

3 Pour the taco seasoning into the ground beef. Pull the ground beef off the heat once the seasoning is mixed in (approximately 3–4 minutes).

4 Place the tortillas on the griddle for 30 seconds to a minute to warm.

5 Once warmed, build the burritos: layer the queso dip, ground beef, shredded cheddar cheese, sour cream, Spanish rice, tortillas strips, and tomatoes.

6 Fold in the sides about 1 to 2 inches (2.5 to 5 cm) inward and roll up the burritos.

7 Once ready, place the burritos on a cleared area of the griddle and place a grill/griddle press on top of the burritos (do not apply pressure if using a cast iron press). Continue to cook until the tortillas begin to turn a light golden brown. Flip and continue to cook on the second side.

8 Pull the burritos and place on a plate for serving. Enjoy!

Pressed Grilled Cheese Burrito

SERVINGS: 4 burritos | **PREP TIME:** 10 minutes | **COOK TIME:** 10–12 minutes

Okay, so here we are. This is a cook that has lived on in infamy here at the Backyard Diner. We both recall the first time we made these Pressed Grilled Cheese Burritos and how we laughed when we took our first bite because it was THAT good!

2 tablespoons (28 g) vegetable oil

1 pound (455 g) 80/20 ground beef

1 packet (1 ounce, or 28 g) taco seasoning

4 burrito-size tortillas

1 cup (208 g) queso dip (We like Tostitos Queso Blanco Dip.)

1 to 2 pounds (455 to 900 g) shredded cheddar cheese (to taste)

4 tablespoons (60 g) sour cream

1 package (5.6 ounces, or 160 g) of Spanish or Mexican rice, prepared

Crispy tortilla strips

1 large tomato, sliced

Note: A heavy cast iron or other large grill/griddle press is best suited for use with this sandwich.

1 Turn the griddle on to medium/low heat (300 to 325°F [150°C to 170°C]).

2 Once the griddle is to temperature, lay the oil on the griddle.

3 Add the ground beef. Cook until browned (approximately 4–5 minutes).

4 Pour the taco seasoning onto the ground beef. Pull the ground beef off the heat once the seasoning is mixed in (approximately 3–4 minutes).

5 Place the tortillas on the griddle for 30 seconds to a minute to warm.

6 Once warmed, build the burritos: layer the queso dip, ground beef, shredded cheddar cheese, sour cream, Spanish rice, tortilla strips, and tomatoes.

7 Fold in the sides about 1 to 2 inches (2.5 to 5 cm) inward and roll up the burritos.

8 Once ready, place the burritos on a cleared area of the griddle and place a grill/griddle press on top of the burritos (do not apply pressure if using a cast iron press). Continue to cook until the tortillas begin to turn a light golden brown. Flip and continue to cook on the second side.

9 Once both sides are lightly browned, lay down some shredded cheddar cheese on the griddle. Lay the burritos on top of the cheese and let them sit for approximately 1 minute (or until the cheese is melted on). Lay a second layer of cheese on the griddle in front of the burritos and flip the burritos onto the second layer of cheese.

10 Once the cheese has melted onto the burritos, pull and place on a plate for serving. Enjoy!

Moons Over My Hammy Copycat Pressed Sandwich

SERVINGS: 2 sandwiches | **PREP TIME:** 10 minutes | **COOK TIME:** 10 minutes

A friend once said, "No one goes to Denny's; they just end up there." Well, if they end up there, most likely someone is ordering the Moons Over My Hammy sandwich. This homemade version is even better. So now you can say, "No one ever goes to Denny's for Moons Over My Hammy—they just come home."

4 eggs, cracked and whisked in a bowl

½ teaspoon salt

½ teaspoon pepper

2 tablespoons (28 g) butter, divided

½ pound (225 g) sliced deli ham

4 slices sourdough bread

4 slices American cheese

4 slices Swiss cheese

Note: A heavy cast iron or other large grill/griddle press is best suited for use with this sandwich.

1 Turn the griddle on to low heat (200–250°F [93–120°C]).

2 Once the griddle is to temperature, sprinkle salt and pepper into the eggs, lay 1 tablespoon (14 g) of butter on the griddle, and slowly pour the whisked eggs onto the butter. Cook until the eggs begin to bubble and are cooked on the bottom and then begin to fold the eggs in. Once they are cooked through, divide the eggs into 2 piles and pull the eggs and set aside.

3 Turn the griddle up to medium/low heat (300 to 325°F [150°C to 170°C]).

4 Once the griddle is to temperature, separate the ham into 2 even stacks and place on the griddle. Cook until the bottom begins to slightly brown and then flip each stack, cooking until the second side is also slightly browned. Place each ham stack onto the piles of eggs.

5 Lay the remaining butter on the griddle and place all 4 slices of bread on the butter.

6 Place the slices of cheese on the bread (American cheese on 2 slices and Swiss cheese on the other 2 slices). Place the ham and eggs on the slices of bread with the Swiss cheese. Top with the remaining slices of bread, laying them American cheese–side down.

7 Place a grill/griddle press on top of each sandwich and lightly press for about 1 minute or until the bottom slices of bread are golden brown.

8 Carefully flip and repeat the same cooking process on the second side.

9 Pull, cut each sandwich in half, and serve with your favorite breakfast side dishes. Enjoy!

Cheesy Vegetarian Pressed Sandwich

SERVINGS: 1 sandwich | **PREP TIME:** 10 minutes | **COOK TIME:** 4 minutes

Simple and fresh, this pressed vegetarian option is more filling than you'd think! It's so packed with flavor, it's destined to become the new healthier selection in your recipe rotation.

½ tablespoon olive oil

1 bag (10 ounces, or 280 g) of fresh spinach leaves

1 tablespoon (14 g) unsalted butter

2 slices sourdough bread

2 slices Swiss cheese

4 slices vine-ripened tomatoes

½ teaspoon salt

½ teaspoon pepper

6–8 slices fresh avocado

1 tablespoon (14 g) mayonnaise

Note: A heavy cast iron or other large grill/griddle press is best suited for use with this sandwich.

1 Turn the griddle on to medium/low heat (300 to 325°F [150°C to 170°C]).

2 Once the griddle is to temperature, lay the oil on the griddle, followed by the spinach.

3 Cook the spinach in the oil, moving the spinach around, and cook for approximately 2 minutes (the spinach will reduce by more than half the original size). Pull from the heat and set aside.

4 Lay the butter on the griddle and move it around in a circle until fully melted on the surface. Place the slices of bread in the melted butter.

5 On 1 slice of bread, place the 2 slices of Swiss cheese, followed by the spinach, tomatoes, sprinkled with salt and pepper, and the avocado.

6 On the second slice of bread, spread the mayonnaise and place mayonnaise-side down on top of the sandwich.

7 Place a grill/griddle press on top of the sandwich and cook for about 1 minute or until the bottom slice of bread is golden brown and the cheese begins to melt.

8 Carefully flip the sandwich and repeat the same cooking process on the second side.

9 Pull from the heat and cut in half. Serve and enjoy!

Classic Turkey Club Panini

SERVINGS: 1 sandwich | **PREP TIME:** 5-7 minutes | **COOK TIME:** 6-8 minutes (20 minutes if including bacon as part of the cook)

We remember when our sister first got a panini press, and we were blown away by the flavors of a pressed sandwich. This Classic Turkey Club Panini was one of our first ever, and it's still one of our favorites!

2 slices bacon

1 tablespoon (14 g) butter

2 slices white bread

2 slices deli sliced turkey breast

1 tomato slice

½ teaspoon salt

½ teaspoon pepper

1 slice Swiss cheese

Note: A heavy cast iron or other large grill/griddle press is best suited for use with this sandwich.

Cook the bacon:

1 Turn the griddle on to medium/low (300 to 325°F [150°C to 170°C]).

2 While the griddle is warming, place the strips of bacon on the griddle. (We have found that placing the bacon on the griddle before it is hot helps keep the bacon from curling too much.) Cook the first side until browned and flip.

3 Continue to cook until the bacon is done to the desired crispiness. Pull and place on a paper towel–lined plate to drain off excess grease.

Cook the panini:

1 Bring the griddle up to medium heat (350°F [180°C]).

2 Once the griddle is to temperature, lay down a pat of butter and move it around in a circle until fully melted on the surface.

3 Place 1 of the slices of bread on the melted butter, followed by the turkey breast, bacon, and tomato. Once the tomato is placed, sprinkle with salt and pepper, lay the Swiss cheese on top, and place the second slice of bread. Place a grill/griddle press on top of the sandwich, without putting pressure on it.

4 After the bottom slice of bread is golden brown, lay down another pat of butter and flip the sandwich over. Place the grill/griddle press back on top of the sandwich.

5 Once the bottom slice of bread is golden brown, pull the sandwich. Serve and enjoy!

Pressed Pastrami on Rye Stacks

SERVINGS: 1 sandwich | **PREP TIME:** 10 minutes | **COOK TIME:** 6–8 minutes

We never thought that simply stacking hot pastrami and Swiss cheese on rye bread would be this good. But when we added one of our favorite dressings and then pressed it to grilled perfection, it turned out better than good. It turned out great!

1 tablespoon (14 g) unsalted butter

2 slices marbled rye bread

1 tablespoon (14 g) mayonnaise

1 tablespoon (11 g) yellow mustard

4 slices Swiss cheese

5–6 slices deli sliced pastrami

Note: A heavy cast iron or other large grill/griddle press is best suited for use with this sandwich.

1 Turn the griddle on to medium/low heat (300 to 325°F [150°C to 170°C]).

2 Once the griddle is to temperature, butter 1 side of each slice of the marbled rye and place 1 of the buttered slices of bread on the griddle. Spread ½ tablespoon of mayonnaise and ½ tablespoon of mustard on the bread and add 2 slices of Swiss cheese.

3 While the bread is toasting, place the pastrami on the griddle and cook each side for 20–30 seconds to get hot. Place the pastrami on top the Swiss cheese and top with 2 more slices of Swiss cheese. Spread the remaining mustard and mayonnaise on the other slice of bread (non-buttered side) and place on top of the pastrami, butter-side up.

4 Once the bottom slice of bread is toasted to a golden brown, carefully flip and place a grill/griddle press on top of the sandwich and press and hold for about 1 minute. (You could also use a large spatula.) Continue cooking until the second side is golden brown and the cheese is completely melted. Serve it up hot and enjoy!

Pressed French Dip Sandwich

SERVINGS: 2 sandwiches | **PREP TIME:** 10 minutes | **COOK TIME:** 7–10 minutes

Whenever we go to a restaurant that serves a French dip sandwich, it's tough NOT to order it. Learning how to make a simple version of our own was one of the best cooking decisions we've ever made.

2 tablespoons (28 g) unsalted butter, divided

½ yellow onion, sliced

½ pound (225 g) deli sliced roast beef

4 slices Swiss cheese

2 French baguettes, sliced

½ cup (120 ml) prepared au jus

Note: A heavy cast iron or other large grill/griddle press is best suited for use with this sandwich.

1 Turn the griddle on to medium/low heat (300 to 325°F [150°C to 170°C]).

2 Once the griddle is to temperature, lay 1 tablespoon (14 g) of butter on the griddle, followed by the onions. Sauté the onions in the butter until the onions become translucent (about 5–6 minutes) and move to the side (off the direct heat).

3 Place the deli sliced roast beef in single layers on the griddle to lightly brown, approximately 30 seconds, and flip. Let sit for 30 more seconds and then pile the roast beef into 2 even stacks and place 2 slices of Swiss cheese on each stack.

4 Place half of the onions on each of the stacks and place each stack into a baguette. Lay the remaining butter on the griddle and move it around in a circle until fully melted on the surface. Place each sandwich on the melted butter and place a grill/griddle press on top. Press for about 1 minute and carefully flip the sandwiches and press again.

5 Pull once each side is lightly browned. Serve with the side of au jus. Enjoy!

Cuban Pressed Sandwich

SERVINGS: 4 sandwiches | **PREP TIME:** 20 minutes (plus additional time to cook the Cuban Marinated pork) | **COOK TIME:** 8-10 minutes

The *Cubano* or Cuban sandwich is one of our favorites. From tangy, to savory, to sweet . . . all of these flavors will explode in your mouth with each bite. Once you have the Cuban Marinated Pork prepared, you'll easily be able to make these scrumptious sandwiches for the masses!

8 slices deli sliced ham

2 tablespoons (22 g) mustard

1 pound (455 g) Cuban Marinated Pork, shredded (See recipe on page 125.)

8 slices Swiss cheese

Dill pickle chips, for topping

4 Cuban rolls, sliced in half

1 Turn the griddle on to medium/low heat (300 to 325°F [150°C to 170°C]).

2 Once the griddle is to temperature, lay the ham on the griddle and heat each side for about 30 seconds to a minute.

3 Spread a thin layer of mustard on the inside of the Cuban rolls. Layer a generous amount of Cuban Marinated Pork on the bottom half of each roll.

4 Place 2 slices of ham on top of the pork, followed by 2 slices of Swiss cheese, and top with pickle chips (add as many or as few as desired).

5 Place the top Cuban rolls on top and place on the griddle. Using a grill/griddle press or a large spatula, firmly press down on each sandwich for 2–3 minutes or until the bottom roll is toasted. Gently flip the sandwich and repeat the same cooking process on the second side. The sandwiches will flatten considerably as the hard Cuban rolls are pressed.

6 Pull and slice diagonally, corner to corner. Serve and enjoy!

If toasting the buns: While the griddle is coming up to temperature, spread the mayonnaise on the inside of the top and bottom buns and lay them on the griddle facedown. Pull the buns when they are a light golden brown and set aside.

Cuban Marinated Pork

2 tablespoons (28 ml) extra-virgin olive oil
1 cup (235 ml) sour orange juice (*naranja agria*)
2½ tablespoons (26 g) Usual Suspects Seasoning
  (See recipe on page 111.)
1 teaspoon dried oregano
7 garlic cloves, minced
1 pork shoulder roast (3 pounds, or 1.4 kg)
½ cup (120 ml) water, for cooking

1 Mix all the ingredients together and place in
  a large resealable plastic bag along with the
  pork shoulder. Marinate at least 6 hours (up to
  24 hours) in the fridge.

2 After the pork shoulder is marinated, remove
  from the fridge, and add the entire contents of the
  plastic bag to a pressure cooker along with ½ cup
  (120 ml) of water.

3 Cook according to the manufacturer's instructions
  for approximately 2 to 2½ hours, until the pork can
  easily be pulled apart and shredded.

The Ultimate Gourmet Grilled Cheese Pressed Sandwich

SERVINGS: 2 sandwiches | **PREP TIME:** 10 minutes | **COOK TIME:** 6–8 minutes

Just when we thought our grilled cheese couldn't get any more gourmet, we went and came up with this multi-cheese option that is so over the top, it is the absolute epitome of #perfection.

2 tablespoons (28 g) unsalted butter

4 slices white mountain bread, or any thin sliced white bread or sourdough bread

10 slices smoked gouda cheese (5 slices per sandwich)

4 slices provolone cheese (2 slices per sandwich)

4 slices Swiss cheese (2 slices per sandwich)

2 cups (225 g) shredded sharp cheddar cheese

Note: A heavy cast iron or other large grill/griddle press is best suited for use with this sandwich.

1 Turn the griddle on to medium/low heat (300 to 325°F [150°C to 170°C]).

2 Once the griddle is to temperature, lay the butter down on the griddle and move it around in a circle until fully melted. Place the slices of bread on the melted butter.

3 Once the bread begins toasting, place the slices of smoked gouda, provolone, and Swiss cheese on 2 of the slices of bread.

4 Place the other 2 slices of bread, with the toasted side up, on top of the cheese.

5 Continue cooking until the bottoms are golden brown.

6 Flip and place a grill/griddle press on top of the sandwiches and cook the second sides until golden brown.

7 Pull the sandwiches from the heat and lay 2 piles of the shredded cheddar cheese (about a half cup [58 g] each) spread out on the griddle and place each sandwich back on each stack. Cook for about a minute or until the cheese is melted onto the sandwiches and begins to form a golden crust.

8 Lay 2 more piles of cheddar cheese, flip each sandwich onto the piles, and repeat the same cooking process on the second side.

9 Pull the sandwiches when to the desired doneness (about 2–3 minutes total time for both sides). Let cool. Serve and enjoy!

Turkey Bacon Ranch Wrap

SERVINGS: 2 wraps | **PREP TIME:** 10 minutes | **COOK TIME:** 12–15 minutes

When we are looking for healthier options, this one right here is one of our preferred recipes. It totally satisfies while ensuring you don't kill your calorie count, especially if you substitute a low-fat or low-carb tortilla.

4 slices bacon

2 spinach tortilla wraps

4 slices Swiss cheese

½ pound (225 g) deli sliced turkey breast

¼ cup (60 g) ranch dressing

Note: A heavy cast iron or other large grill/griddle press is best suited for use with this sandwich.

Cook the bacon:

1 Turn the griddle on to medium heat (350°F [180°C]).

2 While the griddle is warming, place the strips of bacon on the griddle. (We have found that placing the bacon on the griddle before it is hot helps keep the bacon from curling too much.)

3 Cook the first side until browned and flip.

4 Continue to cook until the bacon is done to the desired crispiness. Pull and place on a paper towel–lined plate to drain off excess grease.

Prepare the wraps:

1 On your spinach tortilla wraps, place 2 slices of Swiss cheese and place half of the turkey breast and bacon on each. Squeeze ranch dressing on top.

2 Wrap the tortillas: Fold in the sides of each tortilla about 1 to 2 inches (2.5 to 5 cm) inward. With the sides still folded in, use your thumbs to pull the tortilla flap closest to you and lift it up and over the filling. While rolling the tortilla up and over the filling, keep the tortilla relatively tight and continue to roll until the wrap is secure.

3 Place the wraps on the griddle and place a grill/griddle press on top of the wraps. Let sit for about 1 minute or until the bottoms begin to turn golden brown. Flip the wraps and repeat the same cooking process on the second side.

4 Pull the wraps and cut in the center diagonally. Serve and enjoy!

CHAPTER 4

SMASHING
BREAK-
FASTS

THE RECIPES

The Hungry Hussey's Mashed Potato Cakes

MAKES: 5-6 cakes | **PREP TIME:** 10 minutes | **COOK TIME:** 8-10 minutes

The One and Only, Matthew "The Hungry Hussey" Hussey, shared this recipe, and it is as amazing as it is easy! Thank you for sharing this one, brother!

2 cups (450 g) leftover mashed potatoes

2 eggs

¼ cup (31 g) all-purpose flour

¼ cup (40 g) diced yellow onion

2–3 chives, diced

¼ cup (30 g) shredded cheddar cheese

2 tablespoons (28 ml) vegetable oil, for griddle

OPTIONAL:
sour cream, for topping

1 Mix all the ingredients well until evenly mixed.

2 Turn the griddle on to medium heat (350°F [180°C]).

3 Once the griddle is to temperature, lay the oil on the griddle and scoop ½ cup (120 ml) of the mixture onto the griddle, repeating until the mixture is all gone.

4 Cook for about 3–4 minutes on the first side or until golden brown.

5 Flip and lightly press and continue to cook until the second side is golden brown. (The potato cakes should resemble cooked pancakes.)

6 Serve with some sour cream or your favorite condiment. Enjoy!

Everything Bagel Breakfast Smash

SERVINGS: 1 bagel sandwich | **PREP TIME:** 10 minutes | **COOK TIME:** 15 minutes (20 minutes if including bacon as part of the cook)

"Yup, this one's happening today!" We present to you the Everything Bagel Breakfast Smash!

2 slices bacon

1 everything bagel

1 tablespoon (14 g) butter

4–5 ounces (115 to 140 g) ground sausage, formed into a loosely packed meatball

1 slice American cheese

1 egg

½ teaspoon salt (to taste)

½ teaspoon pepper (to taste)

Note: A heavy cast iron or other large grill/griddle press is best suited for use with this sandwich. You'll also need parchment paper.

Cook the bacon and toast the bagel:

1 Turn the griddle on to medium heat (350°F [180°C]).

2 While the griddle is warming, place the strips of bacon on the griddle. (We have found that placing the bacon on the griddle before it is hot helps keep the bacon from curling too much.)

3 Cook the first side until browned and flip. Continue to cook until the bacon is done to the desired crispiness. Pull and place on a paper towel-lined plate to drain off excess grease.

4 Cut the bagel open, butter the insides, and place on the griddle for 30 seconds to 1 minute until light brown and lightly crispy. Set aside.

Cook the bagel sandwich:

1 Once the griddle is to temperature, place your sausage meatball on the griddle. Let sit for about 30 seconds. After 30 seconds, place a piece of parchment paper on top and press down with a grill/griddle press and hold for 10–15 seconds.

2 Take a spatula and flip the sausage patty over. Once flipped, place the American cheese on top and let it start to melt. After 30 seconds to 1 minute, pull the patty and place on the bottom bagel. Break up and place the bacon on top of the patty.

3 Clear the excess sausage scrap and collect the leftover grease or lay down a pat of butter for your egg. Crack the egg and open it onto the griddle, trying not to break the yolk. Once the egg white becomes opaque, carefully flip the egg and add salt and pepper. After 30–45 seconds, pull the egg and place it on top of the bacon. Place the top bagel on. Serve and enjoy!

Pressed Breakfast Sliders

SERVINGS: 3 sliders | **PREP TIME:** 10 minutes | **COOK TIME:** 15 minutes (20 minutes if including bacon as part of the cook)

Looking for a great way to change up breakfast? This is a fun, easy cook that will have the family asking for it every weekend.

3 eggs

1 teaspoon salt

1 teaspoon pepper

6 slices bacon

6 frozen breakfast sausage patties, defrosted

3 slices American cheese, divided into smaller squares

OPTIONAL:

2 tablespoons (28 g) butter

6 King's Hawaiian Rolls

Note: A heavy cast iron or other large grill/griddle press is best suited for use with this sandwich. You'll also need parchment paper.

Prepare the eggs:

1 Crack each egg into a bowl, add salt and pepper, and whisk until evenly mixed. Set aside.

Cook the bacon:

1 Turn the griddle on to medium heat (350°F [180°C]).

2 While the griddle is warming, place the strips of bacon on the griddle. (We have found that placing the bacon on the griddle before it is hot helps keep the bacon from curling too much.)

3 Cook the first side until browned and flip.

4 Continue to cook until the bacon is done to the desired crispiness. Pull and place on a paper towel–lined plate to drain off excess grease.

Cook the sliders:

1 Take your sausage patties and place them on the griddle. Place a piece of parchment paper on top and press down with a grill/griddle press and hold for 10–15 seconds. Take a spatula, start to scrape, and flip the patties over. Once flipped, place the American cheese on top of each patty and let it start to melt. After 30 seconds to 1 minute, pull the patties and place on the bottom rolls. At this time, you can place the bacon on top of the patty, breaking it up and laying it down side by side.

2 Clear the excess sausage scrap and collect the leftover grease or lay down a pat of butter for your eggs.

3 Slowly pour the beaten eggs onto the griddle. After 30–45 seconds, fold the egg, continue to cook until the eggs are no longer runny, and then pull and place it on top of the bacon.

4 Place the top roll on. Serve and enjoy!

Pressed Breakfast Burrito

SERVINGS: 4 burritos | **PREP TIME:** 10 minutes | **COOK TIME:** 15 minutes (20 minutes if including bacon as part of the cook)

Here's all your preferred breakfast burrito ingredients, now found in a griddled version! Again, what is it about pressing the tortilla with all the goodies inside that intensifies the flavors?

6 slices thick cut bacon

2–4 tablespoons
(28 to 60 ml) vegetable oil

16 ounces (455 g) mild
ground sausage

4–6 large eggs

½ teaspoon salt

½ teaspoon pepper

2–4 tablespoons (28 to 55 g)
unsalted butter

3 ounces (85 g) canned
Hatch Green Chilis

½ cup (115 g) shredded
Mexican cheese blend

4 large flour tortillas

OPTIONAL:
salsa, sour cream, and
guacamole, for topping

Note: A heavy cast iron or other large grill/griddle press is best suited for use with this sandwich.

Cook the bacon:

1 Turn the griddle on to medium/low heat (300 to 325°F [150°C to 170°C]).

2 While the griddle is warming, place the strips of bacon on the griddle. (We have found that placing the bacon on the griddle before it is hot helps keep the bacon from curling too much.)

3 Cook the first side until browned and flip.

4 Continue to cook until the bacon is done to the desired crispiness. Pull and place on a paper towel–lined plate to drain off excess grease. Break or chop up into small bits.

Cook the burritos:

1 Once the griddle is to temperature, lay the oil on the griddle, followed by the ground sausage. Cook the sausage until browned (approximately 4–5 minutes) and then remove.

2 In a medium sized bowl, beat the eggs and add salt and pepper.

3 Lay down the butter on the griddle and move it around in a circle until fully melted on the surface. Slowly pour the egg mixture onto the griddle, making sure it doesn't run off.

4 Once the eggs begin to cook, gently start to fold the sides in. Continue to fold the eggs for another 30–45 seconds until fluffy and golden yellow.

5 Pour the Hatch Green Chilis into the eggs, add the bacon, sausage, and a ½ cup (115 g) of shredded Mexican cheese and mix it all together until the cheese is melted.

6 Remove from the griddle into a large bowl or plate.

7 Take the first tortilla and place it on a clean, flat surface.

8 Take a large spoonful of the cooked ingredients and place in the middle of the tortilla.

9 Fold the sides in first, approximately 1 to 2 inches (2.5 to 5 cm) in, and then from closest to you, pull

the tortilla over the ingredients and finish rolling the burrito.

10 Repeat until all the ingredients are used.

11 Place the burritos directly on the griddle and place a grill/griddle press on top of the burritos. Cook for about a minute or until the bottoms are golden brown. Flip each burrito and repeat the same cooking process on the second side.

12 Pull and serve with your favorite breakfast salsa, sour cream, and guacamole. Enjoy!

Pressed Monte Cristo French Toast Sandwich

SERVINGS: 2 sandwiches | **PREP TIME:** 10 minutes | **COOK TIME:** 6–10 minutes

Have you ever had a Monte Cristo sandwich? It's one sandwich we must order when it's available at a restaurant. This French toast version is as good, or maybe even better, than the original, and it's so simple to make!

FRENCH TOAST

1 cup (235 ml) milk

2 teaspoons sugar

½ teaspoon vanilla extract

2–3 large eggs

1 tablespoon (14 g) butter

4 slices white bread

MONTE CRISTO SANDWICHES:

4 slices Swiss cheese

¼ pound (115 g) deli sliced turkey breast

¼ pound (115 g) deli sliced ham

2 tablespoons (16 g) powdered sugar

2 tablespoons (40 g) raspberry jam

Note: A heavy cast iron or other large grill/griddle press is best suited for use with this sandwich.

1 Mix the milk, sugar, vanilla, and eggs until fully combined.

2 Turn the griddle on to medium/low (300 to 325°F [150°C to 170°C]) heat.

3 Once the griddle is to temperature, lay down a pat of butter and move it around in a circle until fully melted on the surface. Dredge the bread in the egg wash and place on the melted butter. Cook for approximately 1–2 minutes until it begins to brown. Flip the bread and repeat the same cooking process on the second side.

4 Once the French toast is flipped, place a slice of Swiss cheese on each slice of French toast. Evenly divide the sliced turkey and ham and place each stack on 2 of the French toast slices. Top the stacks with the remaining slices of French toast. Place a grill/griddle press on top of the sandwiches and hold for 1 minute.

5 Carefully flip the sandwiches and repeat the same cooking process on the second side by pressing lightly until the cheese is melted through, ensuring you do not burn the outside of the French toast.

6 Once pulled and plated, lightly sprinkle the powdered sugar over each sandwich and serve with a side of raspberry jam (for dipping the sandwich in). Enjoy!

Acknowledgments

We could not do any of the things we do without the love and support of our families. First, Jennifer Walton and Sherry Sheffield continue to inspire and support us daily. To our kids, Brittany, Angie, Kenzie, Cannon, Parker, and Griffin, thank you for making this life sweeter! Dan Rosenberg of The Quarto Group took a chance on us for this project and he has been more than patient—as has the whole Quarto Group family—and we cannot thank you enough! We especially are where we are as content creators because of our incredible griddle community! To our subscribers, friends, and all the others who have supported us through our YouTube journey, THANK YOU, and GRIDDLE ON!

About the Authors

Adam and Brett Walton, "The Waltwins," are identical twins in their thirties from Florida. Adam is a middle-school teacher in Orlando and Brett is a morning host at an FM rock station in Gainesville. They get together on weekends and cook up a storm, as the many thousands of followers of their YouTube channel WALTWINS know so well. The channel, which they launched in 2017, is devoted almost entirely to outdoor-griddle or "flattop" cooking, and it has garnered tens of millions of video views, making them the most watched and most authoritative sources for learning how to cook on these popular cooking appliances. They have been named YouTube "Creators on the Rise" and they appear frequently on local television in Florida.

Index